Insperience

INSPERIENCE

[
I.N.S.P. I.R.E.

the Exceptional Employee Experience
]

Brian T. Church
and
Phillip Duncan

Trade Paperback ISBN: 978-0-9996646-0-5
E-Book ISBN: 978-0-9996646-1-2

Printed in the United States of America

Table of Contents

Foreword

Insperience, by Phillip Duncan and Brian Church, addresses perhaps the greatest challenge of any organization—inspiring your employees to have joy, purpose, and satisfaction in what they do. In an era when companies are focused on giving the customer the ultimate experience, the authors remind us that this will only occur when a foundation of engaged, empowered, and motivated employees are excited about giving those customers that experience.

Duncan and Church's book is timely. With a revived economy, many metropolitan areas are experiencing labor shortages. Recruiting and retaining a superior workforce is incredibly challenging. Employees are looking for differentiators to set their culture apart. *Insperience* is not about a gimmick or pseudo-psychological fad. It encourages employers to engage your workers' hearts, minds, and bodies around seven key pillars to create a revolutionary culture that maximizes employee engagement and productivity.

The book is filled with stories of organizations who have engaged, empowered, and motivated teams of employees in exceptional ways—i.e., who have succeeded in creating what we call the "Insperience." By the end of the book, we hope that you will be motivated to assess and improve your own organization's Insperience, and you can even test your I.Q. (Insperience Quotient) with an online assessment.

Some of the closing lines in the book sum it up well: "There is never a bad time to enhance your culture. It's time to begin. It's time to do the good work of treating people better."

— Dr. Steve Flatt, Chief Executive Officer,
National HealthCare Corporation

Acknowledgments

Making a case for the importance of a welcoming, positive, and empowering culture is impossible unless you experience such a culture every day. A great many people created a support network that made this book possible.

First and foremost, we thank God, the true author of Insperience.

We are blessed to be married to extraordinary women. From initial encouragement to final editing, they have walked every step of this journey with us. The best of what you will read here most likely came from them.

Kimberly and Mary Alice, thank you for everything you do and everything you are!

To our boys, Brian, Jack, Leo, Jesse, and Cam: we could not be more proud to call you our sons. Each of you is a champion in your own right, and it's an honor for us to be raising world-changers. Find people and passions worthy of your absolute best, then give it every day.

To the incredible team at Experience Global: thank you for your unwavering commitment to the belief that people deserve to be treated well. The inimitable Bruce Loeffler, co-founder and Chief Experience Officer, established a strong foundation during his days as Disney's first Service Excellence Coordinator. He was also the first person to speak the word "Insperience." Danielle Kimmey Torrez, Chief Executive Officer, is the quintessential super-boss—she is steady, committed to excellence, and clear vision, coupled with listening skills and a hunger to learn something new every day. This whole team inspires us.

To every client who has partnered with us over the years: thank you! You have stretched and encouraged us.

PART 1

THE CASE FOR INSPERIENCE

Chapter 1

An Introduction
to Insperience™

Where to begin—that's the question, isn't it? So many organizations and so many people are in search of building relationships, community, and culture that transcends mere vocational engagement. So, where do we start? If we were going to take a step back and re-engineer the perfect culture, community, and environment for our people and our organizations, what would we change? What would we build?

As we wrote in our previous book, *The Experience: the 5 Principles of Disney Service and Relationship Excellence*, we established a pathway for creating exceptional experiences for guests, customers, and patients. In search of the perfect model, we began to realize that a superior customer-experience model was only possible with the right foundation in place. This foundational concept has changed the landscape of how we look at a relational business model.

We call it "Insperience."

What is an Insperience? Insperience is a mindset. It is an internal movement to create a positive atmosphere that manifests through employee loyalty, happiness, productivity, and relationships that last a lifetime. Imagine an ecosystem where positive attitudes and genuine care are the norm, where the paycheck is fair but secondary and carrying the flag of the company is paramount.

No amount of corporate rebranding can replace an ongoing commitment to creating positive, memorable, and amazing encounters for your people. You must commit to creating positive encounters for your employees long before you can expect to create the exceptional for your customers. There are irrefutable laws in physics: wine without grapes, a plane without wings, or a car without wheels will not function. You see, just like in physics, there are also irrefutable laws for relationships. There is a specific set of guidelines and principles that, if applied correctly and intentionally, will transform your organization into something you may have never thought possible.

We have been blessed to train tens of thousands of people around the globe on building business relationships. A question that we love to ask when training and teaching is "What experience are you committed to causing for others?" Think about that for a minute. Seriously. Put the book down for a moment and marinate on that phrase. What is it saying? The question is asking if you are being intentional about every encounter you have with others. Encounters can be bad, or they can be good, but make no mistake: they always leave an impression that lasts forever.

Every encounter creates an experience, a subsequent

impression and, ultimately, a mindset. Ask yourself this: "Am I causing positive experiences within and for my organization?"

Our goal in this book is to empower you and your people to enhance the way you think about culture. We invite you to see the difference between what some would call employee engagement and what we call an Insperience. We invite you to think intentionally about the internal experiences you are causing on a daily basis. If you do this, your organization will reach relational, fiscal, and even personal milestones that you never thought possible. We have the evidence to prove it!

Take a journey with us as we dig down to the very foundations of simply treating each other better, creating positive encounters, and setting in place what we believe to be the cornerstone of any successful organization: the Insperience!

Chapter 2

The Journey: How to Use This Book

Insperience is a holistic concept, which is to say that it is interconnected or symbiotic. To enhance any area of the Insperience enhances the whole. The failure to address any area jeopardizes the whole. A holistic approach to building an Insperience is the only way to address the complete sequence of variables within the process.

A holistic approach to building an Insperience must contain each of the following:

The Heart

This is the qualitative piece of the holistic Insperience model. This is where engagement happens and where ambassadors are made. Everything your physical body does—every breath, every step, every bite—is an investment in the health of your physical heart. In the same way, every hire you make, training you offer, and benefit you make available is an investment in the heart of your Insperience. A healthy heart is the key to longevity. If the heart is right, the body can be strengthened and the mind illuminated.

The Mind

This is the quantitative, performance piece of the holistic Insperience model. According to Merriam-Webster, the mind is "the element in an individual that thinks, wills, and reasons." We believe that the mind is the collective consciousness and capabilities of individuals within an organization. When a moment of inspiration comes, it is our minds that set about gathering the necessary components to make that vision a reality. Every move we make begins as a command sent out from the mind.

The Body

The passions of the heart and convictions of the mind come to nothing if not paired with the action of the body. Insperience has the power to create wellness, as well as to enhance the heart and mind. It has been proven that happiness not only lowers the risk of heart disease, it also lowers the risk of employee turnover. In short, the investment in the heart and the mind frequently manifest in the wellness of the body.

* * * * * * *

I.N.S.P.I.R.E.

We believe strongly that you cannot force change within an organization. You must INSPIRE it. There are seven principles that make up the I.N.S.P.I.R.E. model.

ILLUMINATE

The introduction of light changes everything. Consider how long it may take you to make your way across a dark room in the middle of the night compared to crossing the same room at midday. How do you introduce "light" and the opening of the mind as a portion of your Insperience? In this section we will make the case for an intentional focus on education and empowerment.

NURTURE

Consider the workplace an incubator. Successful incubators create the right atmosphere, environment, and ecosystem to foster growth and continuing development. Nurture is the commitment to providing the necessary elements for growth and maturity. If you want to grow a company, you must grow your people. In order to grow your people, you must learn how to address and enhance their well-being emotionally, mentally, and physically.

STRETCH

In this section, we will consider the "mindset of more." The purpose of stretching—of challenging yourself to become more than you were the day before—is to increase your reach. What lies beyond your grasp today?

What is it worth to you? What's it worth to your team? Stretching begins with purpose and welcomes the hard work of becoming greater through process.

PURPOSE
We traditionally think of the definition of purpose as a noun, or our "Why?" In this book, we have chosen to consider the definition of purpose in verb form, meaning an intentional action. What are we doing "on purpose"? We will invite you to purpose your heart, mind, and body, setting them into intentional action toward a specific target. The goal is simple: be exceptional on purpose.

INVEST
The goal of investment is a return, and we argue that the best investment you can make is in your Insperience. There are many forms of investment. Which is right for you? Which is right for now? We will share the secret behind making timely and targeted investments and help you identify your "best yes" when it comes to investing in your team.

REWARD
Rewards are a trending topic in the business community, but they can be tricky. They are, by nature, exceptional compensations in recognition of exceptional behaviors. Rewards must be: (1) tied to specific action, and (2) of sufficient value to enhance existing behaviors. How do you identify the activities for which you are willing to

offer additional compensation? How are you presently rewarding your people, and is it having the desired effect?

ENGAGE

It's challenging to change the behavior of someone in another room. Your options are limited. Shout. Bang on the wall. Make a phone call. How do you personalize a message when you can't see the person with whom you're communicating? Engagement is a function of proximity. It is intentionally drawing nearer to your team to gain a deeper understanding, create clearer communication, and display a willingness to lead from the trenches. How are you navigating this in the digital age of online meetings and telecommuting? What hinders your ability to engage your team, and what value would you find if you removed those obstacles?

Remember that each item we discuss as being part of the Insperience builds on the one prior, but also on the ones that succeed it. Insperience is a formula for the exceptional employee experience and is only made possible through the sum of its parts.

Insperience in Action: We have scoured the business landscape to find prime examples of Insperience and the I.N.S.P.I.R.E. model in actual business practice. In each section, we provide glimpses into how the masters of Insperience engage the heart, mind, and body of their people. The purpose of sharing these company snapshots is not to replicate these examples but rather to use them as inspiration. We will show you specifically how to engage your people's heart, mind, and body when addressing each of the principles by providing in-depth research, quotations, and examples of some of the world's masters at creating the Insperience.

As You Begin
We have created an assessment that can be taken by you alone or by others within your organization. We call it the Insperience Quotient. While it is not imperative that you take the assessment before you read this book, it's important that you determine your starting place.

Insperience architecture must begin at the foundation. Consider this your pre-build site work. You can access this quick assessment here: *www.ExpQuest.com*. Use the Index often! Establish your starting point, but also deploy it every few months to determine your progress. An investment in Insperience must be measurable! This tool, alongside your revenue charts and employee retention graph, will evidence your progress.

The pages that follow will show you how to take an intentional approach to creating an exceptional internal experience. This journey will induce thought, stir ideas, and enable you to build an Insperience model for you and your team.

We want to sincerely thank you for believing that people simply deserve to be treated better. We also want to thank you for coming along with us on this journey.

Enjoy!

Part 2

I.N.S.P.I.R.E.

Chapter 3

Illuminate

Thomas Edison is best known for inventing the modern electric light bulb in 1878 and he was also one of the fathers—alongside Nikola Tesla—of the modern electrical grid. To understand the significance of that technology, we have to remember that, prior to the introduction of the electrical grid, the available sources of light were sunlight by day and gas lamp by night. Light could be enjoyed during the day, but at night, light could scarcely fill a room.

In 1882 Edison introduced one of the first commercial electric grids to the world. Within years, the modern world celebrated gas lamps as romantic but electric power had become a necessity.

Edison's initial conquest, the electric light bulb, exceeded the incumbent technology—the gas lamp—but he wasn't satisfied. His vision was to light up the world. To illuminate is to reveal and, just as Edison evidenced well over a century ago, the light of illumination can travel well beyond its initial contemplation.

So, with that in mind, what is the process for cultivating the concepts of today that will become the construct of the future? How do we grow our people, our brand, and the demand for our deliverables? How do we bring the light to our people and show them the way out of the darkness of ignorance, unpreparedness, and insecurity?

The answer is illumination. Development and innovation require a step into uncharted territory. Darkness, if you will. The decision to travel as a group is wisdom. As you pursue a strategic direction, heed the insights and cautions of your fellow travelers. Allow for "scouts" to run ahead of the group and try new paths— these are your innovators!

Understand that there will be days where you may shine a light only on your next step as a group, but if you travel long enough and develop trust among your party, the light will extend. You will gain ground. An old African proverb states, "If you want to go fast, go alone. If you want to go far, go with a friend."

The secret sauce of illumination is teaching made possible by trust. Consider this: Who would you allow to hold the light for you in a dark room? In business terms, who is prepared and trusted at all levels within your organization to share knowledge, encouragement, and instruction? On the journey to inspire cultural excellence and create an Insperience, your most trusted team members are the ones best positioned to teach. These trusted individuals comprise a safe place where other employees can ask and learn. Consider this quotation by Bob Vanourek, author of *Triple Crown Leadership*: "Trust is built when someone is vulnerable and not taken advantage of." In order to establish trust, there must be vulnerability. A culture that fails to nurture vulnerability experiences diminishing trust. When trust is diminished, we forfeit the opportunity to teach and illuminate. In such an environment, leaders don't inspire—they demand. Their teams do only what is required.

Trust is established through consistency, stability, integrity, and compassion. When those elements are in place, illumination takes the form of education. A hunger for continuing education gives way to expansion. Expansion, built on these foundations, invites individuals to freely envision and create without the fear of failure or the shame of being a disappointment. This is the moment when the light extends into darkness. It is when boundaries disappear and limits are pushed back.

> "The secret sauce of illumination is teaching made possible by trust."

HEART: A PLACE FOR VISION AND HOPE—ACCENTURE

> Poverty is not just a matter of income. We also see a poverty of self-esteem, hope, opportunity, and freedom. People trapped in a cycle of destitution often don't realize that their lives can be changed for the better through their own activities. Once they understand that, it's like a light gets turned on." —*Sir Fazle Abed, Founder of BRAC, a Bangladeshi aid group*

Vision and hope are light for the heart. Cheesy as that may sound, consider how this truth impacts employee retention. In a world where Gallup polls frequently show employee engagement levels hovering around 30%, few companies are worried about "turning on the heart light" (Thank you, Neil Diamond!) for their employees. Most companies leave vision and hope to be worked out in the home and concentrate on finding employees willing to engage their minds and hands in actual work... and it's killing them. It's not too great a leap to say that labor separated from vision and hope would likely result in a high percentage—perhaps around 70 percent—of employees who don't feel engaged.

Allow us to clarify. We are not decrying a lack of corporate vision. What is missing in the lives of most employees today is personal vision. They understand the role they play as a cog in the greater wheel of commerce, but that doesn't extend into their personal journey. The "cycle of destitution" referenced by Sir Abed shows them no way out of where they are now. If there is a glimmer of hope to escape the monotony of the working life, it is only for the few, and so turns the proverbial hamster wheel.

Having now depressed you, our gentle reader, allow us to turn on the lights. Let's talk about a company called Accenture:

- Active clients in over 120 countries
- A leading presence in digital innovation for clients in over 40 industries
- Over 5,000 patents and patents pending in 44 countries
- Partners of record with three quarters of the Fortune Global 500 list

Accenture specializes in all things digital, from strategic and consulting services to organization and tech. They have mastered the art of helping companies continually reinvent themselves in the digital age, and what they are doing for their clients they also are doing for the over 140,000 women who work alongside them.

Accenture has made the intentional decision to lead the charge in empowering women in the workplace, as evidenced in 2015 by their "Being Greater Than" campaign. These were two-minute videos featuring stories of women from around the world who wear the Accenture nametag and are becoming "greater" by pursuing their dreams and breaking down barriers.

Accenture said it this way: "These two-minute videos bring to life our inclusive and diverse culture; our efforts to ensure our people can succeed personally and professionally, and the impact our people are having by giving back to their communities."

Nothing paints vision and opens up possibilities like seeing that something has been successfully done before. Seeing a peer pursuing her dreams and living out her purpose has a predictable result: hope. One thinks: "If she can do it, I can do it!" Even if it doesn't reach the level of complete and actual belief in the end result, people are inspired to try, and that's a big deal.

Before you start thinking this was a one-time inclusion and equality initiative, consider this: Accenture recently set a goal to achieve a completely gender-balanced workforce globally—meaning fifty percent women and fifty percent men—by 2025 and committed to grow the percentage of women serving as managing directors globally to twenty-five percent by 2020.

Why does this matter? Historically, many companies within the tech sector have struggled with recruiting, hiring and retaining women, non-whites, and other underrepresented groups. For Accenture to state their intentions to create gender equality and an inclusive work environment publicly and repeatedly invites accountability. They are willing to be held to the fire for both achieved and unmet goals.

Accenture has sent a message to women everywhere: "You're more than welcome here. You will be celebrated among us. There's room for you at the highest levels. Let's get to work together!" They've turned on the lights by showing (a) what women are already doing to pursue "greater" (b) their commitment to celebrating the victories of their teammates to inspire others and (c) creating more and greater opportunities for women to participate in the industry-leading work for which Accenture is world-renowned.

They broke the hamster wheel and replaced it with a highway.

We began this section with a simple truth: "Vision and hope are light for the heart." Revelation—showing what is possible—leads to inspiration. Inspiration serves as an invitation for the bold to step out and try something. This invitation is followed by education, perspiration, and—given time—the destination.

What are you doing to bring hope to your team? For whom are you actively turning on the light and showing the way out of "stuck" and into action they can get excited about?

The reality is this: when people wake up, they rarely remain in a dark room. The failure to turn on the lights and show a path toward greater will end in the best of your personnel lost to attrition and the rest of your time and resources spent greasing the hamster wheel.

MIND: THE NEXT RIGHT STEP— CHILDREN'S HEALTHCARE OF ATLANTA

"It's as easy as riding a bike!"

Really? Do you ever watch those home-video comedy shows? They seem almost entirely populated by grown folks failing to do things they were able to freely do as children, whether this involves a trampoline, bicycle, or diving board. The fundamentals of riding a bike may not have changed, but the body has! Biker beware!

Whether we're talking about an athlete picking up a ball for the first time in years, a former hair stylist picking up her shears, or a teacher stepping back up to the front of the classroom, starting over is no laughing matter. The fears are genuine and they are many: "What if the game has passed me by? What if I've forgotten everything and they laugh at me?" Suddenly you're right back in the "tween years," having nightmares about going to work in your underwear.

There is a demographic for whom this is a very real, ongoing challenge: young moms. In many cases, moms who came home to be with their children for those early formative years find themselves with five to seven years of invaluable executive experience in the home but struggling to find an on-ramp back into the nine-to-five working world.

Enter: MomForce of Children's Healthcare of Atlanta.

Let's dig in to Children's Healthcare of Atlanta for a moment. First, some statistics:

- 622 licensed beds
- Three hospitals
- The Marcus Autism Center
- 27 neighborhood locations (Seven are Urgent Care Centers.)
- More than 80 telemedicine-presenting sites around Georgia
- More than 50 pediatric cardiologists in 24 locations statewide
- More than 10,600 employees
- Over 2,000 pediatric physicians representing more than 60 pediatric specialties and programs
- 7,000 volunteers

If you're a young mom and there is a medical emergency involving your child, where do you go? The answer: Children's. If there is a Children's Hospital in your area, decision made. There is an inherent trust established because of the level of specialization, both medical and environmental, which Children's offers. They know kids and they know young families.

Now, with that level of trust and goodwill firmly established, what if Children's intentionally reached out to moms to help light the way back into the workplace? What more natural fit could there be?

Hence: MomForce. Designed to help women enter the workforce after an extended absence, this 10-week program allows participants to refresh their skills and build their resumes with meaningful, project-based work. The long-term goal is to provide connections and experiences which will enable moms to re-enter the workforce on a permanent basis.

The program pilot achieved such success that the trial run was renewed for the last three years (and counting). "It's been a welcome on-ramp back into paid employment," says mom of three Katie Fahs.

Keep in mind: Children's Healthcare of Atlanta sees 860,000 patients per year and their commitment to serving the staff who so diligently serve the needs of hurting families is well chronicled. To help their staff manage the stress of such a caseload, they offer wellness retreats, free concierge services, on-site yoga classes, walking trails, and relaxation rooms. For families of their employees, they offer subsidized childcare, $10,000 in annual adoption aid or fertility-treatment coverage, and a parenting network. They take great pride in caring for their own, and yet, in the midst of all of this, they committed to build and *illuminate a path* for a struggling and underserved population.

The mind can be a scary place when it's dark. For those who would seek to advance but can't yet find their way, the imagination can run wild with scenarios of threatening cliffs and villains waiting at every turn. What light can you shine to illuminate their next step? What could you do to clarify or simplify the advancement track within the office? If you've hired well, the odds are very high that the next innovation that will lead to a breakthrough for your company is already in the mind of one of your current employees. How might you light up the landing strip for that individual and that concept to become the next big thing? Perhaps the best way to encourage you to see opportunities for illuminating the mind would be to ask how it has been or might have been done for you.

BODY: COMPLIMENTS OF YOUR ENVIRONMENT—NASHVILLE PREDATORS

Hockey fever is real. Ask anyone who was anywhere near Nashville, Tennessee, in the early summer of 2017, as "Music City" became "Smashville" during the Predators' unlikely run through the playoffs and into the Stanley Cup Finals. The international hockey community and the sporting world at large took notice of the incredible atmosphere created by the 17,000 roaring fanatics inside the downtown arena the Predators call their home on ice, but they had no answers for the tens of thousands filling the city streets and every bar along the infamous "Broadway and Second" and attending watch parties for every game. The entire city, it seemed, had traded their cowboy hats and guitar picks for Predator Gold gear and hockey pucks... and it almost never happened.

The Preds came to Nashville in 1998 and enjoyed a small (by NHL standards) but loyal local fan base. Attendance was good, but rarely great as this traditional Southern community where American football had long reigned supreme became familiar with this newly imported neighbor from the North. Hockey games were fun if you had a free evening and wanted a night on the town with friends, but they weren't must-see TV. The Predators were a local commodity that fed a niche community. In professional sports, this is a recipe for losing money, which is what led then-owner Craig Leopold, in 2007, to sell the franchise to new ownership who had plans to take the team elsewhere. The NHL was leaving Nashville, until... it wasn't. The original purchase deal fell through and, to the surprise of the league and hockey fans everywhere, a group of ten local investors stepped up and bought the team.

The Predators would stay, but everything would change. This is where illuminating the body comes into our story.

Why had the original plan failed? What could this local ownership team introduce that had evaded previous ownership?

The National Hockey League has some of the greatest traditions and most storied franchises in sports. For the fan bases of the Canadian teams, it's a religion. Had the Predators been established in a traditional hockey stronghold, these would have all been understood. The gameplay and cultural expectations would have been transferrable, but this was an expansion by the NHL into a smaller market territory dominated by college football and the NFL. Nashville didn't know hockey.

The club needed Nashville to become a hockey town, but Nashville wouldn't come to hockey. Hockey would have to come to Nashville.

The new ownership accomplished this with a long-term plan that included grassroots marketing campaigns, developing and supporting local youth hockey leagues to build awareness and a future generation of hockey fans, and encouraging the players to plug in to the community. Players in Pred jerseys became regulars at local charitable events and hospitals. Kids were exposed to and subsequently fell in love with the sport. The intimidation factor of witnessing something awesome but foreign diminished, but the work was not yet done. Nashville boasts a unique culture. No stuffy, traditional approach to someone else's game would work.

As the community came to understand more about hockey through the initiatives of the new ownership, the new ownership was re-shaping the team by learning more about Nashville. Instead of competing with and trying to undo years of established sports culture, the Predators began to see themselves as an addition to something that was already great. Tweak by tweak, they reintroduced the brand until Nashville looked unlike anything the NHL had ever seen.

As one example of what that rebranding entailed, consider the Predators' non-traditional approach to their uniforms. The team's rebranding included a complete logo and uniform overhaul in 2011, at which point their dominant color became gold. Shocking, in your face, *cover-your-eyes-because-it's-so-bright* gold. Add to that the piano keys lining the collars and a guitar pick on the shoulder, and you have something uniquely Nashville, but you also appeal to an entrenched tradition of sports in Tennessee. Have you ever seen the University of Tennessee in their home football uniforms? Have you seen the cheering section for UT when they're on the road? Tennessee Orange is not a color that appears in nature. It is a manufactured declaration of "We're here; we're UT!" which fans wear with pride, and that is *exactly* the understanding which guided the design of the Predators' transformation. Attending a home game in Nashville is like diving into Scrooge McDuck's money vault. Gold as far as the eye can see, inside the arena and out. Joe Louis Arena in Detroit may be as red as Superman's cape during a game against the Predators, but the Predator fans who make the trip won't be missed.

Nashville is Music City and the home of country music, so don't be surprised when you are welcomed to the arena with live music, or when some country-music legend appears on the giant screens above your head singing a witty song about the Predators. During the Stanley Cup Finals in 2017, intense local and national interest and debate raged over which legend would be chosen to sing the National Anthem before each home game. Why? Because music is what Nashville does! Music and hockey. Honky-tonks and hockey talk.

Nashville not only became a hockey town; it became the talk of hockey. One writer described it this way: "Behold, this hockey purist's hell: Catfish-tossing from NASCAR fans debating icing calls. Ribbon video boards on every feasible surface that help push revenue. Loud, flashy advertising touting the pillars of middle Tennessee's economy—Nissan, Jack Daniels, Vanderbilt Hospitals and even Goo Goo Clusters. And music. The building's mandate is that if there isn't live hockey at any given moment, there's live music."

Our town. Our team. Our culture. Let's go, Preds!

Let's bring all of this back to illuminating the body. The Predators learned though their initial failure that product availability wasn't enough. What likely would have worked in a different market wouldn't work in Nashville. The city didn't understand what was so great about hockey and hockey didn't get what was so great about Nashville. The question came down to this: could both sides learn? Illuminating the body involves learning how to function in your environment. Businesses who flounder and fail do so frequently because they don't educate and learn from the community. "If you build it, they will come" works great in a baseball movie, but it's a recipe for bankruptcy in business. This must be an inside-out transformation, where each level of the internal culture of an organization (INsperience) commits to becoming something of value to the outside world (EXperience). This commitment is exemplified in a few key ways:

- Commit to communicating effectively with the community you serve, understanding that the largest part of communication is listening.
- Find a group you can educate about your brand and consistently engage, who will become your

biggest fans and ambassadors. (The Predators did this largely through youth hockey.)

- Become the biggest fan of the community that supports you.

Illuminating the body is a process of effective training and education on how to harmonize with, navigate through, and ultimately thrive in the environment you seek to serve.

Chapter 4

Nurture

He's the last one in the operating room... again. Sitting in the silence of a room that, twenty minutes prior, was a whirlwind of activity, the machines have all been silenced and the tools removed to be sterilized and prepped for the next scheduled surgery. Dr. Stanley Dudrick stares at the sheet, angry.

The surgery was a complete success. Every player had performed their role flawlessly. The plan had been executed to perfection and once again, after a "successful surgery," here he was preparing himself to stand before the family, explaining how a successful surgery had failed to deliver their loved one from the operating table. There was no slip of the scalpel, no delay in treatment. The killer was malnutrition. Another patient who, due to their condition, was unable to receive and retain vital nutrition. In a facility where medical miracles happen every day, and the cafeteria serves hot meals around the clock, and in a country where the abundance of food causes more medical issues than scarcity does, how could malnutrition be a cause of death?

There was an answer for this. There had to be. That day in that cold, silent operating room, Dr. Dudrick committed himself to finding it. It was 1964.

It was a few short years later, in 1967, when baby Kelleen, a three-and-a-half-pound newborn baby, arrived at Children's Hospital of Pennsylvania with a congenital anomaly that did not allow her to be fed by mouth. As the medical community scrambled to find a solution, the decision was made to contact Dr. Dudrick and learn more about the treatment he had pioneered—something he was calling Total Parenteral Nutrition. Though completely new and never a attempted on a newborn, what choice did they have but to ask this doctor, who was unwilling to accept what had become an accepted surgical limitation and statistic (death by malnutrition) to work with the Children's Hospital team? Their options were simple. Dr. Dudrick's newfound technique of bypassing the gastrointestinal system by feeding a patient directly through veins or the unthinkable.

Six weeks later—six weeks of setbacks, innumerable tweaks to their approach, and almost constant monitoring—baby Kelleen defied the odds. She weighed in at 6.5 pounds. Her development and growth would continue to be fed entirely via T.P.N. for the next 22 months.

Stanley Dudrick was one doctor positioned to see a need and equipped with the creativity and education to change the standard practice. One doctor who was unwilling to settle for "our best" when the best frequently ended in failure. Now known as the Father of Intravenous

Feeding, he is credited, as of this writing, with saving the lives of over 10 million babies and countless adults.

So, what's the correlation between physical malnutrition and the business world? Consider our present business landscape. The whole world is exposed to your message at the click of a button through social media. Talent in the workforce is strong and abundant. Employee training resources have never been more readily available, and yet signs of malnourishment are everywhere. What does malnourishment, or a failure to nurture, look like in the workplace? Here a few examples:

1. *High Attrition Rates.* As an industry-wide example, consider healthcare. Employee turnover in the healthcare industry in some states is double the national average for turnover in all jobs, according to the Internet Journal of Healthcare Administration. The talent pool in the industry is diminishing and employees in select areas, such as nursing, are *expected* to work long hours for relatively low pay. Poor incentives and outdated management techniques, according to many experts, have led employees to seek work elsewhere. The Saratoga Institute suggests that the average internal cost of turnover ranges from one year's pay plus benefits to two years' salary. Other research indicates figures as high as 150% of an employee's base salary. Attrition is a misappropriation of resources, and it can often be avoidable.

2. *Employee Apathy.* The *Small Business Chronicle* published an article that defined apathetic employees as "... not happy, nor are they disgruntled—they're just there. Employees that have become apathetic typically go through their daily motions at work, doing only the minimum required to complete tasks, remaining detached from their co-workers. These workers are typically uninterested in everything having to do with their workplace, except making money and going home. If a company event is optional or one for which she does not get paid to attend, you will not see the apathetic employee there." They neither provide a spark to the work environment, nor will they receive one, but they serve as representatives of the whole every time they engage a client or coworker. The Gallup organization estimates that there are 22 million actively disengaged employees costing the economy as much as $350 billion dollars per year in lost productivity, including absenteeism, illness, and other low-morale issues. Nothing brings to mind malnourishment quite like a zombie in a business suit.

3. *"Toxic."* It's more than a Britney Spears song. The proliferation of the term itself, and indeed the experience of toxic behaviors among individuals and entire companies, has reached pandemic proportions. Experts assert that as much as 25-30% of the internal environments and external

experiences of companies in America today are in the toxic range. Looking for the telltale signs of toxicity? Try these from a 2015 article by *FastCompany*: (1) unhealthy communication patterns; (2) policies and procedures are non-existent or poorly implemented; (3) toxic leadership; (4) negativity becomes the defining characteristic; and (5) employee health and personal life suffers from exposure.

Most business aren't suffering from a lack of capable crisis management, product expertise, or competitive marketing. They suffer from malnutrition.

Nurture is the immediate and long-term answer for "how." It is specialized care which encourages and enhances growth and development, but specialized care can't be accomplished with general understanding. The level to which we can provide nurture is directly tied to the depth of our understanding. It is both proactive and responsive, providing milk to new additions to your team and the discernment to know when a changeover to meat is appropriate.

Nurture is provision, protection, attention, correction, and praise.

"When we set about accounting for a Napoleon or a Shakespeare or a Raphael or a Wagner or an Edison or other extraordinary person, we understand that the measure of his talent will not explain the whole result, nor even the largest

part of it; no, it is the atmosphere in which the talent was cradled that explains; it is the training it received while it grew, the nurture it got from reading, study, example, the encouragement it gathered from self-recognition and recognition from the outside at each stage of its development: when we know all these details, then we know why the man was ready when his opportunity came."
—*Mark Twain*

> "Nurture is the immediate and long term answer for "how." It is specialized care which encourages and enhances growth and development."

HEART: THIRD PLACE—STARBUCKS

Are you familiar with the concept of a "third place?" Ray Oldenburg introduced the concept in his book *The Great Good Place* in 1989, the concept being that we have (1) home, (2) work, and (3) an "anchor of community life"—a gathering spot. What should a "third place" look like? Oldenburg suggests the following:

- Free or inexpensive
- Food and drink are important
- Highly accessible: within walking distance where possible
- Involves "regulars"—habitual congregants
- Welcoming and comfortable
- Both new friends and old should be found there

Read through those again. Cozy, accessible, somewhere you can meet up and grab a bite or a cup of coffee with a friend... now, try to tell us you didn't just think of Starbucks. There's a great reason for this immediate association. Consider this tidbit from the Starbucks website:

> In 1983, Howard Schultz — then Starbucks' Chairman and CEO — traveled to Italy and became captivated with Italian coffee bars and the romance of the coffee experience. He had a vision to bring the Italian coffeehouse tradition back to the United States. A place for conversation and a sense of community. A third place between work and home.

Starbucks has been busy becoming a "third place" for over thirty years — literally since before the book introducing the Third Place concept was ever written! In an article written for the *dailymeal.com*, Dr. Chuck Schaeffer describes it this way:

> Many people, myself included, have relied on Starbucks as our third place for so long that we get separation anxiety when we realize we can't take our mid-morning walk through this magical, familiar land of free Wi-Fi and seasonal lattes. The irony is that we don't get these feelings because we miss the coffee—or even the Wi-Fi—but instead because we miss the feeling of belonging, safety, and community that companies like Starbucks have worked seamlessly into their homey interiors and sociable employees. Indeed, for people constantly isolated from friends and family due to increasing work demands and pressures, having a third place provides social support and community—even if they're only there to do more work.

Any time you read a review of an establishment where a patron uses the words "belonging, safety and community," you can be sure that someone has grasped the concept of nurturing the heart, but that's a customer describing their *EXperience*. What does Starbucks do in-house, among and for their employees to cultivate an *INsperience* capable of making Starbucks the poster child for the third place? How do they get their employees to buy in? After all, the green apron, for them, represents "second place."

It's work.

The answer lies in the alignment of Starbucks culture with its overall corporate strategy. What separates them from the pack of other purveyors of good coffee is that every encounter with a Starbucks, no matter where you find it, is experiential. There are sights, smells, welcoming faces, and even some "in the know" nomenclature—*Venti?* *Grande?*—that stir familiarity and a sense of belonging immediately for their regulars. But who is responsible for stewarding that experience? How do they keep it consistent across over 24,000 stores in 70+ countries? In short: culture. Insperience.

Starbucks describes their culture as an "Employee First" culture. Their first goal is not to establish a rapport with their regulars, but to instill a trusting and enjoyable work environment for their employees. The friendly banter between baristas as they pass along details of your order is a distinctive of the Starbucks way. To put it simply, their goal is to invert traditional workplace hierarchy. Managers are not barking orders—they are positioned to serve their teams. Regional managers serve the local store managers and on up the chain it goes, with each level committed to empowering and partnering with the other to build a place where they all want to come to work.

Here's the point: Starbucks realized early on that they could never become anyone's third place without a focus on being a great second place. You can't nurture the hearts of your patrons through a warm, cozy, and inviting space when they are sitting just opposite the bar from people shouting at each other, rudely correcting the pronunciation of their sometimes difficult-to-pronounce nomenclature, and engaging in toxic workplace behaviors. Their mission? "To inspire and nurture the human spirit — one person, one cup and one neighborhood at a time." This requires the Heart-level engagement of their team.

Take away the Employee First culture and Starbucks never makes its way out of Seattle. It's just another cup of coffee.

We wonder how many other companies there may be where an internal, employee-facing "heart adjustment" could take a potent, marketable service or deliverable from local legend to international phenomenon?

INsperience will always ultimately determine EXperience.

MIND: UNAPOLOGETICALLY YOU— STEELHOUSE

What feeds your mind? What refreshes you and allows you to perform at your best, with clarity and precision? If you can't answer this question immediately, without having to sit down and think about it, don't fret. Most people, especially most working-age Americans, can't. We can guess at it—throw out suggestions that we may have seen on television or in an ad somewhere—but how many vacations have we gone on only to come home more exhausted? We can easily throw out a list of one hundred things we'd rather be doing than working, but "nurturing the mind"?

It's not that we see no value in nurture. Things like faith, hearth, and home tend to nurture the heart, and we can always turn to the gym and tweak our diet to nurture the body, but what of the mind? It seems, in the absence of finding ways to nourish it, we are content to find ways to simply "turn it off"—hence the proliferation of the term "binge-watching." But what if there were a better way? What if you could create a workplace reality that people weren't constantly scheming up a plan to get away from?

Steelhouse, a performance marketing and advertising team in Los Angeles, has done just that. They have created a competitive, incredibly fast-paced and demanding environment full of people who can't seem to get enough of each other.

The Steelhouse culture is decidedly and intentionally different. Some would say it is "anti-work," seeing as they don't actually track vacation hours or time off. They assign work to specific teams with deadlines and assume that those teams will handle their business in the way they see fit. Why make them punch a clock when the goal isn't a punched timecard but an innovative finished product? CEO Mark Douglas is known for introducing outside-the-box, "anti-work" concepts like Steelhouse Days. Douglas was a firm believer that every month should have at least one three-day weekend, so Steelhouse Days became a holiday of his own creation, filling in the months that didn't have a pre-existing long weekend already on the calendar.

"This guy doesn't sound innovative; he sounds lazy!" you might say. Truth be told, he and his team are anything *but* lazy! They are the fastest-growing advertising company in the country and are churning out iconic work with some of the biggest brands in the world. Whether you agree with the methods or not, things like "Steelhouse Days" and unlimited vacation are examples of the company's mission to trust its employees to the greatest extent possible. FYI: It's more than just time off. Since 2011, Steelhouse has offered $2,000 a year to employees for personal travel.

Douglas and his team have created a culture that has attracted and retained like-minded people. Between 2013 and 2016, only five people (out of 250) left the company, three of whom left for reasons unrelated to the job itself.

Here's why we feel like Steelhouse is on to something when it comes to nurturing the mind:

1. Illuminating the escape hatch. Need a break? Take one. Get away from this for a few minutes, get your head right, then come back and do exemplary work. Deadlines are surely still a part of the culture—this is advertising, after all. But no one is chained to a desk for eight hours a day and instructed to be creative. *The mind uncaged is a mind at rest.*

2. Hiring with the intention to trust. As you may have guessed, getting a job at Steelhouse is competitive, and they hire with the full intention to hand the company's future over to their team. They hire the best, then get out of the way so they can be the best. *The leadership is there to assemble, support and enjoy working with a team of rock stars.*

3. Lead as you would have your team behave. There are rules of business and then there are

principles. The Steelhouse approach seems to be a deep appreciation for the principles, but an utter disregard for the rules. The message to their team is "We operate outside the box." In their world of advertising and marketing, their leadership style is an invitation to their team to join them on the cutting edge. *Leadership behavior speaks louder than leadership language.*

4. The "Norm!" effect. Remember *Cheers*? The theme song said it all: "Sometimes you wanna go where everybody knows your name." Steelhouse initiates and cultivates camaraderie. Their goal has always been to create work from which you need not escape and an environment full of people you would choose to "do life with". *Work among friends is scarcely defined as arduous labor.*

Nurturing the mind doesn't require being "anti" anything. It need not be radical for the sake of being radical, but neither should it be restrained for the sake of being restrained. Nurturing the mind is the freedom to be unapologetically you. What appeals to the demographics that your line of work attracts? Are they free spirits? Penny-pinchers? Cultivate your atmosphere to bring out their best. Empower them to not only complete tasks but to improve upon time-tested techniques that may have become time-wasting antiques! Create an environment where work isn't a word you need to escape from and you will find that work can be the highest form of nurturing the mind.

BODY: GOOD BUSINESS SENSE—
EASTMAN CHEMICAL COMPANY

The party's over. Your daughter's birthday has been celebrated by thirteen—count them—*thirteen* 11-year-old girls who have been in your home now for the past twenty-four hours. Whose idea was this sleepover? You walk the last of the guests to their parents' car, whisper a prayer of thanks, and begin the walk back into your home to assess the damage. Walking in the door, the sight that greets you is one you will not soon forget. How can so much damage have been done in such a short amount of time? Who ordered all of those pizzas, and why could they not have been eaten in the kitchen? Is that glitter on the family dog? You must now answer one inescapable question: someone has to clean this up and the entire family has mysteriously disappeared, so where will you begin?

Cute story, but have you ever been in that paralyzed place of knowing that something must be done *by you* but you have absolutely no idea where to start? When it comes to nurturing the body, the tragic reality is that a considerable percentage of the people you walk past on a daily basis are living this moment of emotional paralysis every day. They know that changes must be made in their physical health but they have no clue where to begin. Obesity statistics are staggering. Tens of thousands of people make the decision every month that they are going to make a positive change in their diet and activity levels, but immediately upon making the decision *to* do something they are faced with the question of *how* to do it. Unsure of where to begin, for many that initial question serves as the hurdle they never overcome.

When it comes to nurturing the body, more and more companies are stepping up to the challenge of providing a path for their people to overcome health challenges. Why? It may seem crass, but the health of their people has direct implications on the health of their bottom line. With soaring medical costs and the cost of sick days piling up, gone are the days of dancing around the taboos of healthy weight management and behavioral health, but the situation remains delicate. No one wants to live in or lead a nanny-state scenario where you dictate everything to your team! So how do you do it?

Let's take a look at Eastman Chemical Company and their approach to nurturing the body of their employees. Eastman is a global producer of more than 1,200 chemicals, fibers, and plastics with over 10,000 employees around the world. The challenges they faced in rolling out a health initiative were considerable. How do you mobilize an incredibly large employee population with varying cultural influences who are spread around the world?

Eastman's approach began with this statement: *In order to build a culture of health we had to first build relationships with our internal Eastman manufacturing and functional organizations. Because of these relationships we have been able to form division wellness teams and site steering teams...*

Because Eastman began the *how* of their health program with an intentional approach to relationship-building, their people were ready to embrace the program when it rolled out. Engaging teams in the process began with listening and trusting their teams to know what they needed and partner with them to make a great plan. Thus, both leadership and the rank-and-file employees of Eastman agreed that health and wellness needed to become just as important as on-site safety. Was this relational approach successful? Of the 8,691 Eastman employees eligible for the health promotion program, 7,637 (88%) participated. We'd say that's a pretty huge win.

Eastman's health improvement program, offered to employees and their spouses, included:

- Health-risk assessments
- An e-health platform
- Onsite biometrics screenings and health advising
- HealthE-Living—onsite, face-to-face health coaching
- Physical activity programs—six onsite fitness centers and three onsite group fitness studios, Walk this Way, Eastman Triathlon, Boot Camp, and 60+ group fitness classes weekly
- Health promotion and wellness programs— screenings, Weight No More, Lunch 'n Learns, Health Improvement Programs
- Weight-management programs
- JOBFIT data management and outcomes— injury prevention, worker conditioning, back health, and physical abilities testing for pre-employment within specific organizations.

- Shift-worker programming
- Telephonic stress-management program

Does it make good business sense to nurture the body of your employees? In 2010, an ROI study for Eastman demonstrated a $3.20 return for every dollar invested in the program after just three years. When taking incentives into consideration, Eastman saw a $3.62 return for every $1.00 spent on the program, *with a total medical and drug claims savings of $6.38 million.*

Yes. Done well, with the right approach and the buy-in of your team, it makes a great deal of business sense to Nurture the Body, but take it one step further. Nurture, at its core, is not a "What's in it for me?" behavior. Let's take off our business glasses for a moment. What impact did Eastman's decision to pursue improving the health their employees have on the home lives of their people? How many moms and dads were granted the energy to interact differently with their children, and how many people were freed from suffering the effects of symptoms related to behavioral choices—diet, inactivity, etc.?

Eastman made available the gift of health—a gift which extended far beyond any spreadsheet or Business ROI. A gift like this changes relational dynamics. Don't for a minute think that Eastman employees will ever forget it. The decision by leadership to contend for the health of Eastman employees, engaging them relationally and empowering them—and their spouses—to make positive changes in their health converted employees to ambassadors.

Chapter 5

Stretch

Throughout the 1980s and early 1990s, Derek Redmond was a big deal in British track and field. He was a key player in the 4x400 relay team that had stunned the world by outpacing the U.S. in the World Championships of 1991. So when he pursued individual 400m glory in the 1992 Olympics in Barcelona, the whole kingdom was watching.

He prepared himself mentally and physically, as he had done so many times before, and finally the time came to set his feet in the blocks for the semifinal race. Some 65,000 people jammed the stadium to watch as the gun sounded and Derek sprang out among the leaders, but in the gentle curve of the 150m mark everything went wrong. Derek will tell you that he heard his hamstring pop over the din of the crowd. He knew his race was done before he ever reached the ground.

The physical pain, though immense, was drowned out only by the rush of emotions that years of preparation and determination had built up. It wasn't supposed to end this way. Derek Redmond was a champion. A finisher.

So, Derek got up.

The other runners had long since crossed the finish line, but all eyes were now on the 155m mark. Hobbled, in obvious pain, but with a determination that would not allow him to go home without finishing what he had started, Derek crossed the 170m mark... 200.

Watching from the stands, inspired by his son, Jim Redmond was stirred to do what *he* had always done. He made his way through the stunned crowd, forced his way past security, and charged to his son's side. Video footage from that day shows Jim Redmond in full protection and support mode, unwilling to allow anyone or anything to stand in the way of his son's mission to finish well.

And finish he did. Finish *they* did.

By the time the race was over, Derek Redmond was known far beyond his island. The 65,000 people in the stands roared his name. The whole world was watching and cheering him across the line, and indeed the whole world continues to watch. Video footage online has measurable hits of over 100 million views, and Derek now enjoys his role as a much sought-after motivational speaker.

Derek Redmond was constantly striving for more. It was the defining characteristic of his track-and-field career. That belief drove him to practice for years before anyone in the track-and-field world ever knew his name, and made him *stretch* day after day to become more. That belief in "more" compelled Derek, an acclaimed member of an incredibly accomplished relay team, to stretch into the vulnerable world of running an individual event.

Derek knew all too well, as he lay on the track at the 150 meter mark, that he wouldn't be hailed as the fastest man in the world in the 400m. Unwilling to settle for less, his mindset of *more* allowed him to establish in a moment a new and non-negotiable goal.

We contend that stretching is a mindset. There is always more, always greater, and those who would be great are hardwired to perceive and pursue. As easy as it is to focus on the heroics of Derek Redmond in our story, did you notice how he finished? He finished aided and accompanied by his father. When those who are ready to grow and achieve get into action, that is the time to have mentors and coaches ready within your organization. Who are the mentors and coaches? Those who have pursued *more* in days past. Stretching is a cultural distinction!

Within your team's culture, what is inviting the best and brightest to step outside of their comfort zone? Having assessments which help you identify the outliers and mentorship that is calling forth exceptional qualities in individuals is essential. Stretching without coaching can feel reckless. It flies in the face of self-preservation, unless it is loudly and intentionally encouraged.

Stretching must be encouraged but also constrained. What is the *more* for which your team will give one hundred and *ten* percent? Aligning the personal goals of your team—advancement, increased pay, innovation—with your business goals will serve as a guardrail to keep everyone moving in the same direction. Stretching without a target can lead to distraction or reek of desperation.

Finally, stretching assumes change and there are no guarantees. How does your existing culture handle change? Would your employees say that failure is fatal or an opportunity for redirection? Consider the consequences associated with coloring outside the lines. If your team fears the repercussions of getting outside of the box, enjoying a cultural distinction of stretching—pursuing the *more*—is not possible.

A mindset which embraces the concept of stretching and being stretched is essential for any manner of measurable growth. When stretching is embraced, then every setback becomes a reinforced portion of your foundation. Every innovation, breakthrough, and victory become a high-water mark of achievement and the new target to be surpassed.

Consider this: Had Derek Redmond's day ended perfectly according to his design with him holding the gold medal, who would remember him outside of the track-and-field community in Great Britain? Not the 65,000 in the stands. Certainly not the millions who have been inspired and stretched by videos and stories told of his courage.

Stretching is risk. The only guarantee is that without it your best days and those of your team are behind you.

> "There is always more, always greater, and those who would be great are hardwired to perceive and pursue it."

HEART: THE BEST OF THE STORY— SOUTHWEST AIRLINES

Who is your favorite person on the planet? If we were to sit down with you over a cup of coffee and ask you why you're so fond of them, how would you begin? An amazing thing happens when we have an opportunity to share about things or people we love. There is a physical transformation that takes place... a softening. Sitting there enjoying our coffee, how long would it be before a hint of a smile came over your face and you began telling us a story?

There is a special place in the human experience for story. Robert McKee said it this way: "Stories are the creative conversion of life itself into a more powerful, clearer, more meaningful experience. They are the currency of human contact."

It's not surprising, then, that a section of his book that is dedicated to stretching the heart would point to a company that has mastered the art of storytelling.

A man was en route from a business trip in Los Angeles to his daughter's home in Denver to see his three-year-old grandson for the last time. The boy, beaten into a coma by his mother's live-in boyfriend, was being taken off of life support at 9 p.m. that evening so his organs could be used to save other lives. The man's wife called Southwest to arrange the last-minute flight and explained the emergency situation. Unfortunately, the man was held up by LA traffic and long lines at LAX and didn't make it to the gate on time. When he finally made it there, 12 minutes after the plane was scheduled to leave, he was shocked to find the pilot waiting for him. He thanked the pilot profusely and the pilot said, "They can't go anywhere without me, and I wasn't going anywhere without you. Now relax. We'll get you there. And again, I'm so sorry."

Sorry for the emotional haymaker, but this is one of one hundred stories we could have chosen from the "Southwest is Amazing" file. No one is surprised when they hear that the team at Southwest has taken yet another opportunity to create a uniquely personal experience for their air travel guests, but here's what may surprise you: most of those stories you've heard were not intended for your ears. Perhaps you've seen some of the amazing YouTube videos that get shared all over social media about Southwest? Most of these were also not originally intended for you.

A large majority of Southwest's masterful storytelling was not created so that we would fall more deeply in love with them. It's how they pass on, internally, the DNA of caring. It's to remind the people of Southwest what it means to be Southwest.

In 2013, Southwest released a bold new vision and purpose statement. The vision statement read: "Our vision is to become the world's most loved, most flown, and most profitable airline." That vision flowed from the statement of purpose, which read, "We exist to connect people to what's important in their lives through friendly, reliable, and low-cost air travel." Linger here for a moment and consider what Southwest is setting out to do and what they are asking of their employees.

Most loved?

Most flown?

Most profitable?

Connect people to what's important in their lives?

So much for just taking tickets and handling bags.

It was during this season of transition and renewed focus that Southwest identified story as the best possible vehicle for conveying and keeping top of mind their vision and purpose statement.

Who told the stories?

Southwest started at the top. Gary Kelly, Southwest's CEO, would offer what he called a "shout out" every week to employees who were going above and beyond for their coworkers and passengers. *Spirit*, the employee magazine published by Southwest, got in on the act as well, featuring story after story of amazing employees taking service excellence to another level. The company began looking for reasons to hand out awards for exceptional service, and each award was accompanied by ceremony and fanfare complete with— you guessed it—stories of what had been done to merit such an honor. Then came the master stroke of genius that began with the *Southwest Airlines: Our Purpose and Vision* video.

Stop for a moment. Take out your phone or your computer and spend a few minutes actually watching that video. Don't assume you know what it's all about.

Experience it.

Now, imagine that you are an employee of Southwest. How do you feel? You must feel like Superman, because that's how the men and women of Southwest responded! They took on the identity of "best in class" for experiential air travel. Because of the stories they were told about who they were and the company they were a part of, they became a team capable of accomplishing the vision and purpose set before them.

Southwest mastered the art of telling their story, but the secret of their success was their target audience. Southwest knew that the public would never hold a high opinion about them or their service that their team did not first hold of themselves, so they began to establish a sense of identity and pride in being a part of the Southwest family. Once their team believed themselves to be extraordinary, they were willing to offer no less to their clients.

A heart that has been stretched is one that looks at the opportunities set before it and believes that more and better is not only possible but probable. "More" is who they are. It is a matter of identity. *Empowering the heart moves hesitant minds and stubborn feet.*

Don't miss one essential element—Southwest's vision and purpose were about business. These statements were unapologetically about profitability and being the best in the air, but their vision required the buy-in of the

Southwest team. Southwest's rank-and-file employees' belief in the vision and purpose would be the runway. If leadership had failed to instill through storytelling that sense of Southwest "Best in Class" identity, the plane would never have gotten off the ground.

Stretching the heart of your team creates the capacity for greater, so what's your story? How does the story you're telling internally among your team compliment your vision and purpose? There are stories from your past, about your present team and opportunity, and the vision for your future that will make your team come alive.

Tell those stories well, and tell them often.

MIND: TEAR DOWN THAT WALL!— SALESFORCE

People, as a rule, have a great deal of appreciation for our personal contribution to any collective body of work, but in most cases our contribution alone can't produce the ultimate goal. That's where "Stretching the Mind" comes in. How do we make room for recognizing the value of the people and processes that, when placed alongside our work, create our deliverables?

Every person in your office is paid to be there. Each hire, at every level from maintenance to management, was intentionally chosen as one whose contribution could move your company one step closer to profitability and excellence. How does that strike you?

Depending on your experience with your coworkers, you are either in wholehearted agreement or you are questioning the sanity of the one who brought in **insert list of names here**.

That questioning of value, whether it be directed at an individual or a department, is fertile soil for all the wrong sorts of fruit. In an environment where there is no intentional focus on unity and appreciation for diversity of thought and experience, tribalism becomes the standard. "Our part" of the process displaces the finished product as the focus. The protection of sacred cows — habits, rights, and "border protection" schemes — takes the place of generating profits.

Allow us to prove this via a ridiculous example from outside the office. Enter the "fitted sheet." Someone with no hand in putting sheets on the bed or the folding of laundry may hear those two words spoken and, after a pause, say "Yes? What about them?" The laundry czar of the home, however, will hear those words and shudder. In their experience, fitted sheets rank just below child hunger in their list of favorite things. Why? Because folding them neatly requires hours of YouTube research and the fitted sheet for your mattress has to be "just so." Too big or too small and you wake up with your face on a 22-year-old mattress. Worst of all, the non-laundry members of the family complain constantly. "What's wrong with these sheets? How hard can this be?"

Imagine if, out of sheer frustration, the decision is made to simply forego the fitted sheet altogether and just require everyone to sleep on an exposed mattress. What would happen?

Chaos. Immediate and utter chaos.

How can this situation be remedied? The answer has nothing to do with the sheet. The sheet is what it is—a necessary part of the process of making a proper bed. What could be added, however, is understanding. The non-laundry parties can be invited to participate in the folding and the spreading of the hateful fitted sheets, creating understanding and empathy for this portion of the process and possibly allowing for creative insights on how this enemy might be overcome.

Back to the business world. How do we create a culture that embraces and celebrates the process beyond our own "to do" list? Let's take a look at how SalesForce does it.

When Mark Benio founded SalesForce he introduced a management practice called V2MOM—Vision, Values, Methods, Obstacles and Metrics—which he required each member of his executive team to produce and publish. These documents were to list out their departmental goals and priorities for the year.

Once completed, these manifestos went into the hands of every department leader in their charge, who would then create their own V2MOM and pass both documents on to their staff and personnel. Ultimately, all of SalesForce had their own personal V2MOM aligned with the goals of their senior leadership and every level of management in between. They had a clearly established and communicated plan, informed by knowing what their leadership was measuring and pursuing.

This practice effectively eliminated the "class system" division between levels of management simply because each clearly stated their directives, what they were measuring and what success looked like.

Another tool employed by SalesForce is their own in-house training and culture tool known as "SalesForce Trailhead." Using their own engagement platform, this began as the go-to place for employees to develop new skills and prepare themselves for advancement by broadening their knowledge base. This video game-like, non-threatening approach to training on everything from job skills to culture and leadership development became so popular that it is now a feature available to the general public to refine their skills and learn how to better use SalesForce's innovations. They made learning about the broad scope of their work fun. So fun, in fact, that it became a product in itself.

We should remind you here that Stretching the Mind involves getting beyond yourself, expanding your understanding of the whole enterprise. The higher you climb in management, the greater that understanding must be. Creating this engaging, non-threatening platform which so effectively reflects the SalesForce culture encourages participation in that stretching process. A culture that embraces the stretching process of understanding the work of the whole increases greatly the pool of candidates for advancement from within.

Another thing SalesForce is known for is opening the lines of communication with their team. Town hall meetings are an essential part of the culture, but the format may surprise you. These are not gatherings where the leadership ascends the pulpit and speaks to the little people. Quite the opposite, actually. The goal is for leadership to speak 25% of the time, leaving three fourths of the meeting for leadership to hear from and answer to the rank and file. Questions are wholly unscripted as are the responses, which results in a powerful level of trust.

Before you think that no one would ever talk about the really hard stuff in a Town Hall setting, SalesForce has that covered through the Chatter group known as "Airing of Grievances." (If this is not hilarious to you, take a moment and YouTube *Seinfeld Festivus.*) Nothing is off limits, so long as you are willing to make a suggestion on improvement or receive direct help for the issue you raise.

Finally, SalesForce is committed to creating opportunities for cross-departmental engagement, the highest form of which is the KOA Club. Any employee, regardless of department or title, who has been with the company for ten years or more, is made a member of this esteemed group, and life in the KOA Club is sweet. Every year the founders of the company hold a special two-day celebration in San Francisco where members enjoy time together serving the community, attending black-tie event, a special Town Hall just for them and senior management, and so much more. When the Warriors were playing in the NBA finals, KOA Club members were treated to game one at the Oracle Arena in box suites. Not a bad way to bring your people together!

Stretching the mind is at the core of expansion, both personal and corporate. That stretching boils down to two fundamental elements: *increasing understanding through clear communication* and *encouraging engagement and collaboration among your team,* which is best evidenced and taught from the top down.

If you're not sure how well your company is doing in this area, the most common evidence of a culture that has stagnated is tribalism. Tribalism's message is simple: be surrounded (blend in), be safe (don't be exceptional), and be still (move only when necessary—never move first).

Compare this with the benefits of creating an environment which emphasizes the stretching of the mind: we collaborate (communication), we innovate (create new paths), and we accelerate (calculated risk born of trust).

BODY: EXTENDING YOUR REACH— CHURCH OF THE HIGHLANDS, ALABAMA

Stretch your arms out as wide as you can. Reach as far forward and as high as your body will allow. Imagine that the most precious thing in your life—be it a possession or a loved one—is in peril just beyond your fingertips, and you'll come face to face with a difficult reality. Our physical influence has limits. We can only affect so much before we must either receive help or consider what's beyond our reach a loss.

Difficult realities often lead to difficult questions, and this is no exception. If the reality is that my personal physical influence is limited, then the question becomes, "Am I willing to lose what is beyond my reach?" Do I manage only that which is within my sphere or is there more available to me? In business terms, your existing team is a limited resource. Do you manage within your existing capabilities, or do you expand?

Stop for a moment. Before we proceed and consider this concept of stretching the body, let us first make something clear—bigger is not always better. Some boundaries and barriers are in place for your protection, and it is wisdom to take the time to discern the purposes and principles behind your desire to grow. Each employee you add is a stretch! You don't have to open a new branch to stretch your body! Expansion involves risk. Count the costs, then you'll be able to stand firm on being excellent within your existing sphere and intentional growth.

Let's establish some helpful and healthy guidelines to stretching the body and extending your reach:

1. *Define "Why"*: What are you reaching for and what is it worth to you?
2. *Define "When"*: Have you maximized your existing sphere?
3. *Define "Who"*: Will your resources support your existing sphere and the investments required to expand?

4. *Define "the Win":* When we accomplish this, we will...

Let's step into the nonprofit world for a little change of pace and meet the Church of the Highlands. As we look at what they've accomplished and how, please understand that the language and measurables we will share are consistent with their purpose and mission as a Christian church. With fairly humble beginnings in 2001, Church of the Highlands has grown to average more than 38,000 people attending services each weekend, with campuses spread across the state of Alabama. How? Check out this excerpt from their website:

> Our purpose at Church of the Highlands is "To reach people with the life-giving message of Jesus that they might become fully devoted followers of Christ." We filter every idea, program, and budget request through our purpose statement. If what we plan doesn't help us meet our purpose, then we don't do it.

If we place this purpose statement alongside our guidelines for expansion, we'll see that their purpose is a declaration of pursuit. Everything they do is about reaching people with a specific message, so if someone is beyond their reach they are, by mission, committed to expansion. Why? Because of the value of both their message and the one they would reach with it.

With this purpose statement as a foundation, Senior Pastor Chris Hodges—with considerable help from the initial Dream Team of 34 people committed to seeing this dream become a reality—established the Church of the Highlands on February 4, 2001. That Sunday, more than 350 people attended the first service. In their first year, the church grew to 600 people in weekly attendance, but keep in mind that growth for the sake of growth wasn't the purpose. Within that growth there were 371 people who responded to the message and committed their lives to Christ. At the same time—in their first year—they helped plant six other churches and gave nearly a quarter of their income to missions.

Consider these statistics for the first ten years of Church of the Highlands (2001–2011):

- Expansion to eight campuses across the state of Alabama
- Over 5,000 services held
- 2,966 baptisms
- Missions giving in excess of $10,000,000
- A role in over 190 church plants worldwide
- 22,420+ decisions for Christ

How did they do it?

First: They maintained a singular focus on their purpose. They engaged only the people and processes which were consistent with their purpose from day one. That's a principle which was written into their purpose statement! If it didn't help them reach the next person, it didn't get on the radar.

Second: The message and the messengers. How do you support 38,000 parishioners every weekend across the state? The people you reached become the people who are reaching—each one fed becomes one who feeds. In church terms: discipleship. Church of the Highlands employs a consistent curriculum called the "Growth Track" across all congregations. Here's what they say about it:

> The Growth Track is made up of four steps that equip you to (1) connect to the church; (2) discover the strengths of your purposeful design; (3) develop your personal leadership; and (4) use your God-given gifts to make a difference in the lives of others.

Third: Consistency. The experience created at the Church of the Highlands, no matter which campus you attend, is simultaneously unique to the community it serves and yet completely "Church of the Highlands." Each campus is assigned a Campus Pastor and a staff to support the local church, including live worship in each location prior to Pastor Hodges's message being beamed in remotely on a big screen. Each campus hears the same message, but is greeted by equipped members of their community. Consistent branding and signage is used across all campuses so that you always feel at home when you're amongst the Highlanders. The ethos of the Dream

Team is passed, link by link, person by person, as they continue to reach for the lost.

Let's bring all this back to you. Stretching the body is equipping and empowering new voices to carry the message to extend your reach. You are creating and empowering a human chain, extending into areas you could never have reached alone. Success in this venture lies in understating the distinction between "stretching the body" and transferring the responsibility. This is not a handoff of the mandate to reach people, but a partnership between multiple locations who share a common purpose, mission, and principled process. Church of the Highlands has mastered the art of equipping members of their family to share their purpose and pass on their cultural DNA.

Stretching the body only makes sense if what you desire most is beyond your reach. If you find it necessary to get beyond yourself, consider this: whomever you trust to extend your reach must share the value with which you hold the prize. They will handle it first. If yours is to be a venture that stretches beyond your current reach, establish a culture that is led to lead and fed to feed.

Chapter 6

Purpose

Spend an afternoon with a group of school-aged siblings and you will inevitably hear, usually in a loud and accusatory tone, "You did that on purpose!" Apparently, the concepts of premeditation and intent are a part of early childhood development, falling somewhere just after "No!" and "Mine!"

Let's consider the concept of purpose in its verb form as adults. In other words, what are we doing "on purpose"? To purpose is to approach a course of action with determination, commitment, and a decided heart. It is the art of being unwaveringly intentional. This begs the question, "What in our business deserves that level of scrutiny and commitment?" John Mackey of Whole Foods Market said this: "If you are lucky enough to be someone's employer, then you have a moral obligation to make sure people look forward to coming to work in the morning."

From Amazon to Zulily, the consensus is clear. The highest return for your purposed attention is your culture. It is your Insperience.

"Doing Culture On Purpose" indicates two commitments.

Commitment #1 is an understanding and embracing of the fundamentals of your work. It's the "Gentlemen, this is a football" moment that coaching legend Vince Lombardi would have at the beginning every season during his long tenure as head coach of the Green Bay Packers. The more intentional the focus upon fundamentals, the less time you spend repairing, retooling, and rehiring.

What are the fundamental pillars of your business? How are you intentionally reinforcing those activities and inspecting the support and resource lines in those areas? Having established the stability of the ground floor, what activities must then take place, performed by whom and in what order, to build the structure the "outside world" will see?

It's imperative when building culture that people be empowered to do and serve well. The tendency is to look beyond the fundamentals and discount their impact on culture, jumping ahead to the flourishes and "fun stuff," but it's a proven fact—losing isn't fun in any area of life. Vince Lombardi understood that a locker room that wasn't established on the fundamentals of blocking, tackling, and fair play would be a locker room full of losers.

So you embrace the fundamentals. You empower and educate your staff. Now what?

Commitment #2 is to add the differentiators. This is where you intentionally add into the mix the qualities over and above technical proficiency that will become the hallmark of your service and the pride of your staff. This is where you say goodbye to your competition.

As one example of purposed attention in the area of your company's culture, let's consider gratitude. When we walk through our consultation and facilitation processes with business owners and executives, we always ask what they perceive is missing from their culture. We then ask a sampling of employees the same question in an anonymous interview setting. Would it surprise you to learn that one of the most common responses we get from both sides is gratitude?

> "To purpose is to approach a course of action with determination, commitment, and a decided heart. It is the art of being unwaveringly intentional."

Consider the results of this 2013 gratitude survey conducted for the John Templeton Foundation by the polling firm Penn Schoen Berland:

- Upwards of 90 percent of the 2,000 people polled agreed that grateful people are more fulfilled, lead richer lives, and are more likely to have friends.

- Ninety-three percent of those polled agreed that grateful bosses were more likely to be successful.
- Eighteen percent thought that grateful bosses would be seen as "weak."
- Bosses were placed in the category of "never" being thanked by 35 percent of those polled.
- "Your current job" ranked lowest on the list of things for which people were grateful.
- For some perspective, people earning annual salaries over $150,000 ranked "gratitude for your job" right alongside "your right to vote."
- Of all the places people were likely to express gratitude, workplaces ranked dead last despite the fact that those same respondents wished to be thanked more often at work.
- Less than 15 percent of those polled express daily gratitude to friends or colleagues.
- When asked about "most people today," people said gratitude levels were declining—only 19 percent selected the option that most people today are "more likely to have an attitude of gratitude than 10 or 20 years ago."

The question, it seems, boils down to this: why should anyone thank you for doing your job? And why should you ever thank your coworkers for doing what they get paid to do? And why thank your boss when he's the one making the most money? Here are a very few simple reasons why a purposed approach to something as simple as gratitude as a differentiator makes sense:

- Gratitude is rocket fuel for motivation. According to Globoforce's Spring 2014 Workforce Mood Tracker survey, 86 percent of employees who were recognized at work felt more motivated in their jobs.
- Gratitude promotes retention. Globoforce's Spring 2012 Workforce Mood Tracker study found 80 percent of those who felt appreciated at work wanted to stay at the company.
- Gratitude promotes physical and emotional wellbeing. Studies indicate gratitude among one of the positive attributes that contribute to everything from better sleep to a stronger immune system.

The fundamentals allowed you to introduce the differentiator, and the differentiator made all the difference. Differentiators come in many forms. Some, like gratitude or authentic service, apply in every industry and at every level. Others are industry specific. Gather your leadership, both from management and the trenches, and identify what the differentiators are in your sphere. Price, quality of ingredients, accessibility—which additives complement your focus on the fundamentals and the skillset of your team?

Identify the right course of purposed action through conversations with your leadership team and the

Insperience Quotient. Lock on to your target with determination, commitment, and a decided heart, then be unwaveringly intentional about mastering the fundamentals. Once that foundation is established, enjoy deploying the differentiators.

What you have "Purposed to Do" you will achieve by doing things on purpose. Your time and talent will be protected by a firm foundation and your focus can be given to growth and intentional expansion.

HEART: THE HEART OF WHAT MATTERS—KIMPTON HOTELS AND RESTAURANTS

Imagine this scene: Neil and his girlfriend Amanda are out sharing a wonderful New Year's Eve. This is the third year in a row they have rung in the New Year together, complete with the traditional kiss at the stroke of midnight, but this one will be special. Neil has a ring in his pocket. As their friends crowd the television to watch the ball drop, Neil pulls Amanda away.

Ten... nine... eight... Neil drops to his knee... seven... six...five... he asks the question... four... three... Amanda covers her mouth in shock...two...one... Amanda gets out her laptop and begins, without yet having answered the question, to make a spreadsheet of all the pros and cons of this partnership, complete with a full DNA-informed mock-up of what their children might look like.

Seriously, Amanda?

Purposed action that impacts the heart is not meant to be contemplated; it must be felt. In terms of Insperience, this is the opportunity for the employer to indicate to the employee that they hear them, understand and value their life outside the walls of the company, and support their personal vision and mission.

As an example, let's take a look at Kimpton Hotels and Restaurants. Set in your mind the breadth of employee demographics of the hospitality industry. From the kid taking his first job bussing tables a few hours a week to the seasoned hotel staff veteran and on up through the executive suite, how does a corporation serve this diverse a population with perks that say "We see you" and "We honor you"?

If you spend some time reading through the Kimpton perks and benefits, you will quickly discover that they are all about family. They go above and beyond for new parents, offering up to six weeks of paid parental leave for mothers, fathers, and partners—which is well above the industry standard. (Note: this leave is available for parents welcoming new children through adoption or live birth.) From the moment you welcome your little one, Kimpton treats them as their most honored guest.

If you're a little further along the childrearing process, Kimpton has you covered. Consider "Bill's Honor Roll," which was developed by leadership at Kimpton to give encouragement and recognition for the children of employees who have put their heads down in the classroom and achieved high academic success. When a child's name is added to Bill's Honor Roll, they receive a personalized note of congratulations from CEO Mike DeFrino and a gift certificate to Amazon or Barnes & Noble.

Stop for a minute and consider what it must be like for a mom or dad to put that envelope into the hand of their child. "Susie, check it out! You got mail today!" What better way is there to endear yourself to a parent than to honor their child? Think of the impact on the children! Think of how proud they are when they come to visit mom or dad at work. How many kids have brought the note from their good friend Mike to show to mom and dad's friends at the office?

This is brilliant stuff, but Kimpton isn't done.

Continuing their theme of honoring the family, Kimpton offers back-up care for children and elderly parents. Every salaried and hourly eligible employee who is a primary caregiver for their children or elderly parent is offered back-up care. No more last-minute scrambles when you get the dreaded "I can't make it to watch Johnny this morning" text. Kimpton's got you covered.

Feeling a little burned out? Need a break? Kimpton's general managers, executive chefs, and home office and regional employees of director status or higher receive one month of paid sabbatical leave for every seven years of service. There is, however, a catch to this perk. They must unplug completely from their jobs. No work email and no business-related phone calls during their sabbatical.

Kimpton is winning the hearts of their people by employing policies and perks that say, "This matters to you, and you matter to us." It's been a win for Kimpton in the form of incredible employee loyalty, which has led to consistent excellence of service for guests of both their boutique hotels and restaurants. The investment pays off when happy guests go out of their way to tell their friends about their experiences with Kimpton staff. The question, then, is, *How are you doing when it comes to intentionally speaking to the hearts of your employees?* Is the message being intercepted by the minds of your team, where they try to work out why you are making these changes and what angle you might be working, or are your efforts being met with reactions of the heart? If you're reaching the heart, you will see genuine gratitude. The equation, if the heart can be broken down in such terms, looks something like this:

- Purposeful heart touch from company to employee is met with gratitude.
- Consistent touch creates sustained gratitude, which results in increased retention.
- Touch + Gratitude + Retention = Affection.
- Employees who get to the level of affection for their work and the culture in which they serve are what we refer to as Ambassadors. Employee Ambassadors identify themselves as a part of something that is altogether worthy of their best and serve accordingly.
- Your team of Ambassadors at their best = happy customers, referrals, and revenue.

MIND: WHERE APPROACH MEETS IDENTITY—MORGAN MOTOR COMPANY, UNITED KINGDOM

The power of the human mind is...well, mind-boggling. When a moment of inspiration comes and our hearts are all aflutter it is our minds that set about gathering all of the necessary components to make the heart's vision a reality.

We're concerning ourselves with "purposing our mind," which is not the *act* of thinking but *how* we think. Our mindset, or approach to making sense of the world around us, establishes our behaviors, which in turn establishes our habits. These habits, over the course of time, build and become our legacy.

Here's the reality: when it comes to culture, "how to" is superseded only by "why." A non-negotiable "why" is essential, but it can't do the work on its own. If you have no established approach or method of operation, your "purpose" is little more than a preference.

Allow us to introduce you to Morgan Motor Company, a little car company in the UK with which you may not be familiar, but for whom, by this chapter's end, you will share our enthusiasm. Every Morgan is and has been for one hundred years coach-built. Handcrafted. But before you start getting pictures of Pinewood Derby cars in your head, know that every car that rolls off the line is subject not only to current safety standards but also to the performance and beauty standards with which the

Morgan brand is associated. Built in a classic style with the great lines and grace of the automobiles of old, these things can move and they look good doing it.

The city of Malvern, where the factory is located, is quintessentially British. It's a picturesque postcard of small-town life in the old country, and about seventy percent of the workforce—with an average age of forty-two—lives in Malvern itself. From the factory line to the pub, the grocers to the ball fields, the 180 skilled craftsmen who make up the Morgan Family truly "do life together".

Stop for a moment and consider the complexity of the modern car. The electrical systems, the quality and safety metrics that must be passed, and the reliability we have come to expect with every turn of the key. If you haven't done so yet, take a quick moment to look up Morgan Motor Company on your browser and take a look at what they're creating and remind yourself: handcrafted. This is, and has been for over 100 years, high art. In an increasingly automated world, how do they find the craftsmen to do this?

In a word: apprenticeship.

Morgan takes great pride in its apprenticeship program. Sheet metal. Machine shop. Wood shop. Trim shop. Paint shop. Each area of manufacturing is populated by laborers who are, above all else, teachers and learners, masters and apprentices.

Do the math on a one-hundred-year-old company that has an average employee length of stay of twenty-five years and you'll realize quickly that Morgan doesn't lose people very often. There is a sense of pride and ownership that goes into making each car that leaves the factory— that each car that bears the name "Morgan" is a direct reflection on its makers.

Prospective owners are encouraged to visit Malvern and watch their car being built. They can walk the factory floor and select their paint colors and leather trim packages. They can decide if the back of their rolling personal statement will feature a spare wheel or a luggage rack. They are invited to become a part of the custom creation process, adding their own individuality to the Morgan way. They are adopted into the Morgan family.

In an era where most of the automotive industry is pursuing more and more automation, Morgan has established a standard for which they will not apologize and from which they will not deviate. Sure, in some strategic areas they will innovate and modernize, but they are unapologetically Morgan. They are handcrafted excellence. What have you purposed in your mind to be? To become? What distinctive features do you offer? The mindset you adopt regarding your work will serve as the guardrail for your process development, create your culture, and ultimately will shape both your Insperience and your Experience.

Morgan recognized that it's difficult to duplicate random behavior. For every time you "get it right" you will miss the mark a dozen times. It's better to be intentional. It's better to provide a purposed environment that empowers your team through consistency and authenticity, which in turn leads to trust and a shared vision. Morgan accomplishes this by a commitment to apprenticeship. Theirs is not a passion that a car gets built, but that it be built a certain way—the Morgan way. A way that is unconventional, frequently inefficient—compared to "modern methods"—and entirely duplicatable.

The "Morgan Family," as every family does, has unique DNA. That DNA, carried by generation after generation of their employees, is what creates their unmistakable brand.

Momentum can't be gained when there are constant changes in direction. Purposing the mind is the ability to remain on course, despite prevailing winds of second-guessing and distraction. It's an approach that becomes a part of your identity.

A Purposed Leadership Mind results in peace of mind for employees. Removing instability allows for focus, and uninterrupted focus creates momentum.

BODY: PREFERENCE VERSUS PURPOSE— UNITED STATES NAVAL ACADEMY AND WEST POINT

At the risk of alienating some of our readers, we're about to make a bold statement: There is one and only one "must see" rivalry in American college football. Only one game should matter to every American football fan, regardless of where they were raised or where they went to school, and that game is Army versus Navy.

Fear not. This chapter is not about football. This chapter is identifying a culture that exemplifies purposing the body, and there really was no other option for who embodies this more than the Cadets, the Midshipmen, and their coaches. Let's set the table for what students at these institutions face in terms of academics, athletics, and military preparation.

These four-year colleges are effectively Ivy League institutions, with Cadets and Middies expected to carry course loads between 21 and 24 credit hours per semester. Graduates from both schools are enlisted into their respective branches of the military for a minimum of five years, "fast tracked" into military leadership. If you think you or your kids might be interested in applying, you can't. You have to be nominated by someone like a member of Congress or the Vice President of the United States. Even better, ring up the White House and get a letter of nomination from the President. We're not kidding.

Not only are students carrying major course loads academically—these are soldiers in training. From day one on campus they are a part of a military hierarchy and basic training, and no one is exempt. Ever. No days off. Daily exercises are required, where Monday you may enjoy some "live fire" drills after class. Wednesday? How about some light cartography or cryptology? On Friday afternoon, let's zipline across the Hudson River in full battle gear.

All done with classwork and training? Awesome, because football practice starts in an hour. Then film study for an hour, followed by a few hours on the field playing big-boy college football against the highest level of intercollegiate competition. These young men are giants. Emotional, moral, and intellectual giants. They play for the love of the game and the honor of the academy, knowing full well that within in a few short years they will step off of the ball field and onto the battlefield.

Want to be their coach? Would you like to be a member of the staff, primarily comprised of civilians, charged with helping these young men navigate the journey from high school superstars, through a recreation of every sergeant-in-your-face video you've ever seen, and ultimately to battle-ready soldiers who happen to be elite-level athletes? Imagine standing in the middle of a line of graduating seniors, arm in arm after the Army/Navy game as your school song is played for the last time. Think of the bonds that are formed in a crucible such as this one.

These kids could be anywhere, but they've chosen the academy. The same for these coaches. They choose this path because they are elite. Success for them is not dependent upon contract offers from the NFL. These are, as Joe Drape's book says in the title, "soldiers first." They are our best and brightest. They purpose their bodies, both as individuals and as a team, in the classroom, the training ground, and the practice field in preparation for military service.

Great story, but what doesn't this have to do with my business?

In short: everything.

You can't be a cadet or a midshipman "just a little." You're either there on purpose or you aren't there at all.

Cadets and Middies are immersed in their history and they understand why their culture is both precious and non-negotiable—though they probably wouldn't use the word "precious." They represent something important and their contribution—their utmost—is required.

Does that sound like most working environments? How many employees really understand the history of the places where they work? The real-life stories of the sacrifices made to build what they enjoy today? How many truly have connected the trajectory of their future with the level of excellence they will deliver today? Is the "finish line" a race to be *won by one* at all costs, or are they committed to crossing as a team?

Purposing the body can't be evidenced by attendance statistics alone. It's not just the person who "shows up." This is about giving the best you have to offer towards something that matters. A purposed mind without a purposed body is just mental assent. It counts for nothing. A purposed and decided heart without a purposed body is love unspoken. It can never be felt by another or returned.

Not every work environment will stir passions like West Point or the Naval Academy in Annapolis, but can any environment thrive without some measure of passion that stirs decided action? Is there nothing about or to which our people can be fully committed?

Our suggestion is simply this: make it your job to find *it*, first for yourself, and then share it with others. A purposed body committed to decided action has the power to transform three fundamental elements of your business:

- *Retention*—People will stay where their contribution is valued and their work matters to them, particularly in a cohesive team environment.
- *Recruiting*—Knowing what the pillars are for your culture will attract the right prospective employees and empower you to make better strategic hires.
- *Revenue*—Value extended to and felt by employees for their work and about their contribution will become value to end users in the form of excellent service, which increases revenue.

The Army/Navy game is almost never significant when it comes to national title hopes or major bowl bids. It's not a match-up of Goliath versus Goliath, but it is an invitation to participate in the passion of the Cadets and Midshipmen. It is passion personified and called to action.

How is it that these men can give four years of absolute devotion to something as grueling as what we have shared with you and yet employees everywhere are hard pressed to devote eight hours of their day to focused effort? The answer: these Cadets and Midshipmen understand the consequences of anything less than total victory. They fight for their lives in every area of their lives. To purpose the body is to give all, and the simple truth is that most people never make it beyond "It'll do." Sure, we'd like more money. We want to stop saying "Maybe next year" to our spouses and kids, but... there's always next year. If we lose this job, we'll find another.

A body will never be purposed if it is governed by an apathetic heart and mind. Preferences masquerading as purposes aren't worth living or dying for.

This is a call to deep personal introspection. For those of you in leadership, this is a call to *purpose excavation*, both personal and amongst your team.

What do you really want?

What is it worth to you?

What must receive your absolute best to make it available to you?

When you find it, *purpose your body* to it. If it is a true purpose, devote your life to making much of it.

Chapter 7

Invest

In May of 2017, *Money* magazine published an article breaking down the average expense for a family of four to visit Walt Disney World in Orlando. For the average Disney price estimate, they factored in the resort's "standard" dining plan for those staying on site in a moderate Disney hotel at $436.50. The plan wouldn't cover all meals, so an extra $100 per day was added per person for food—and no, that isn't too much for eating inside the parks. For park tickets they chose four days' worth of Park Hopper passes. Travel expenses reflect airfare rates at $350 per person round-trip. Here's what they found:

- Hotels: $1,746
- Transportation: $1,400
- Admission: $1,660
- Food: $1,154
- Souvenirs & Extras: $400
- Total: $6,360

If you spend an average of 10 hours inside the parks, over those four days the cost per hour spent there comes to $39.75 per person—per hour.

Some gentle reader just read those figures and spilled coffee all over themselves. Another read the same data and was immediately transported beyond the sticker price to the memories of their daughter's first encounter with a Disney princess in the shadow of the castle. Their reaction?

"Worth every penny!"

Is it worth it? As a parent, you have to answer a few questions: What is motivating your willingness to invest in this trip? How sure are you that an investment here is your "best yes" based upon your desired outcome? Could you save money and go to a different park and get the same results?

Wise investing is a byproduct of something more intimate than familiarity. Investment devoid of intimate discernment is little more than a wishing well. We maintain that there are three principles that govern wise investing:

1. *A Clearly Defined "Win."* Wise investing is, at its core, a matter of reverse engineering. "This is what we want. In order to have this, these are the things that must take place. In order for these things to happen, these are the positions and processes which must be empowered, eliminated, and created." The absence of a clearly defined target

forfeits the possibility of a bullseye. Note: Not all "wins" are static elements. You may find along the way that you underestimated your team, in which case you will adjust your range beyond your initial plan. Perhaps the season is not yet right for the initiative you've rolled out and there are a few missing pieces, so you adjust from "destination" to "preparation," but in either case you must begin with a fixed "win" in mind.

2. *The Exchange Rate.* Incentivizing movement within your organization begins with your intentions, but it must extend through your understanding of your team. Just as the leader says, "I desire; therefore I invest," the team says, "I desire; therefore I contribute." Understand that those desires are almost never the same. The team member may value the company's end goal, but what they desire is more likely tied to their ability to say "yes" to something within their own home. The exchange rate lies in the understanding of what each party desires. A dangled carrot doesn't motivate a lion.

3. *Timing and Communication.* A poorly timed investment is the essence of distraction, and an investment without strong communication is the essence of waste. Investments necessarily divert focus. A new wireless plan, a *Biggest Loser* health initiative, a book club—each of these very simple examples requires communication from leadership and the attention and response of your team.

Participation requires an exchange on the part of your team members, as their Tuesday lunch break is now reserved for "Books with the Boss" or the office weigh-in and work out. Take these very minor examples of investments and consider the implications of major shifts in company focus, asset alignment, or personnel. Both sides of the equation *must* be positive! Excellent timing coupled with poor communication results in mistrust and office chatter. Perfect communication burdened with poor timing reaps missed deadlines, divided loyalties and confusion. Wise investing requires a keen understanding of seasons and a mastery of action- able communication.

> "Wise investing is a byproduct of something more intimate than familiarity. Investment devoid of intimate discernment is little more than a wishing well."

So let's bring this full circle. If you made the decision today at lunch that you were taking the kids to Disney for the week of Thanksgiving, how would you tell them? When would you tell them?

- *How*: "Hey kids, your mother and I sat down and counted the costs for a trip to Disney. Please open the folder in front of you and take out the spreadsheet labeled 'Travel Expenses'..." *No!* Once the costs have been calculated, the timing established, and the decision made, you communicate the magic. You paint vision. You lay out the "win" for them in the most exciting way you can imagine. As you communicate the magic, you invite them to participate in the vision. You see it and you share it. The more you share it, the more real it becomes.

- *When*: "Hey kids, I know you have exams this week and that Thanksgiving is six months away, but guess what?" Bad plan, unless you're comfortable with the answers on their math final having more to do with Mickey and Space Mountain than multiplication and long division. Add to that the reality that you have now condemned yourself to some one hundred eighty days of "When do we leave?" and a six-year-old who can't sleep because they're too excited. Timing is everything! Share big news when the big news can enjoy the spotlight.

Investment is a measurable indication of the direction you have chosen, the speed with which you plan to travel, and the care with which you have chosen your season and travel companions.

It is, at its core, about return. Unsavory as it may sound, it is about giving to get. We contend that the investment that will yield the largest returns on the balance sheet must always begin with the holistic wellness of your people. Invest wisely in things that your team values and watch their performance, and yours, soar.

HEART: LET MY PEOPLE SURF—PATAGONIA

Investing in the heart is a variation on an old theme: put your money where your heart is. Your people, your cause, your belief. Take that which is of value to you and sow intentionally into these things. This may seem simple, but when you consider how many various hands are reaching into the coffers for "urgent" costs ranging from utilities and services to payroll and insurance, the hand most often left wanting is the one which extends from the heart. Investing in the heart gets pushed to a "When we reach _____, we can do _____."

Companies who invest well in the heart have something of principle and non-negotiable value rooted within their core. It's not an afterthought, but a significant part of their identity.

Consider this: just like the human body, the heart of a company affects every other system. The strongest physical body or the most acute mind with a failing heart has a very short window in which they might be recognized and enjoyed.

If your company enjoys a great reputation, you will attract the brightest and most innovative applicants and new employees. In the same way, a brilliant and proven staff attracts the best and most cunning recruiters. Strong bodies and strong minds are attractive, but it's the heart—the Insperience—that leads to retention. If you find yourself in constant bidding wars to retain talent or forced to replace great people, this is an indication that you may suffer from a weak heart.

Patagonia is unique. Any company which has a standing policy known as "Let my people go surfing" surely qualifies for "outside the box." This policy allows employees in their Ventura, California offices to make a surf run when there is a perfect surf—regardless of the time of day. When the surf report is checked before the stock report, you have evidence of passion.

Patagonia founder/owner Yvon Chouinard wrote the book on this. Literally. It's called *Let My People Go Surfing*. In this book she states:

> If you care about having a company where employees treat work as play and regard themselves as ultimate customers for the products they produce, then you have to be careful whom you hire, treat them right, and train them to treat other people right. Otherwise you may come to work one day and find it isn't a place you want to be anymore. Patagonia doesn't

usually advertise in the *Wall Street Journal*, attend job fairs, or hire corporate headhunters to find new employees. We prefer instead to seek out people through an informal network of friends, colleagues, and business associates. We don't want someone who can just do a job; we want the best person for the job. Yet we don't look for "stars" seeking special treatment and perks. Our best efforts are collaborative, and the Patagonia culture rewards the ensemble player while it barely tolerates those who need the limelight.

We also seek, as I mentioned above, core Patagonia product users, people who love to spend as much time as possible in the mountains or the wild. We are, after all, an outdoor company...We can hardly continue to make the best outdoor clothing if we become primarily an "indoor" culture. So we seek out "dirtbags" who feel more at home in a base camp or on the river than they do in the office. All the better if they have excellent qualifications for whatever job we hire them for, but we'll often take a risk on an itinerant rock climber that we wouldn't on a run-of-the-mill MBA. Finding a dyed-in-the-wool businessperson to take up climbing or river running is a lot more difficult than teaching a person with a ready passion for the outdoors how to do a job.

Of course, we do hire some people strictly for their technical expertise. We have employees who never sleep outside or who have never peed in the woods. What they all do share, as our organizational development consultant noted, is a passion for something outside themselves, whether for surfing or opera, climbing or gardening, skiing or community activism.

With Patagonia, what they do is informed by what they love. They didn't trade in their surfboards and tents for conference tables and coffee breaks. Their innovation is born of continued immersion in the act of doing. Their culture demands a focus on the matters that ultimately touch their hearts and inform their bottom line. Allow us to break that down:

> The best way to innovate and "build a better board" is to take inspiration from the joy of immersing and investing yourself in what you love. Use that inspiration to create marketable products in which other enthusiasts will delight and invest. Take every opportunity to enjoy, advocate for, and participate in what moves you most deeply.

From hiring practices to employee perks and even environmental advocacy, Patagonia is putting their money where their heart is.

So, the question is simple: what's in your heart? What lies at the core of your enterprise? The question may be simple, but the answer may be buried under years of decisions that were made based upon the tyranny of the urgent. The response of many in business would be, "We do this for one reason: *to make money!*" That's fine, but it remains outside of the core.

Making money stimulates the mind and empowers the body, but *why* you invest your time and talent in exchange for money speaks to the heart.

Making money attracts talent. Why you make money allows you to keep it.

Investing in the heart empowers retention.

Everything your physical body does—every breath, every step, every bite—is an investment in the health of your physical heart. In the same way, every hire you make, training you offer, and benefit you make available is an investment in the Heart of your Insperience. A healthy heart is the key to longevity. If the heart is right, the body can be strengthened and the mind illuminated.

MIND: MENTAL BANDWIDTH—ZAPPOS

Mindspace. Bandwidth. "Mental capacity." Call it what you will, we're all blessed with only so much of the ability to see everything that needs to be done, make an actionable plan, and execute. As traffic begins to pile up on the highway of your mind, you begin to experience stress. The more the mental traffic piles up, the higher the stress level. High stress levels will, over time, lead to health complications which—you guessed it—create more stress. If you need convincing with regard to the high level of stress and anxiety in the workplace, consider the following:

- The average commuter in America experiences more measurable stress than that exhibited by fighter pilots and riot police.
- Americans work, on average, two hours longer every day than their counterparts in Italy and Germany while "enjoying" significantly less paid time off than other developed nations.
- A researcher interviewed over one thousand kids, grades three through twelve, and asked: "If you were granted one wish to change the way your parents' work affects your life, what would it be?" The most common answer wasn't about more money or more time, but that their parents would be less stressed out.

Over 30% of Americans "function" on less than six hours of sleep per night. That's the benchmark for sleep deprivation. Why is that a big deal? Take a moment to Google the spooky effects of sleep deprivation. Not good.

Look around your office today and give some real thought to what may be going on in the lives and minds of your people. If you feel as though a lack of focus is having a negative impact on productivity you are *absolutely* right, but there is something you can do to help.

Investing in the mind can take many forms. We could take an entire chapter and talk about innovations in education and new forms of engagement for your staff, but often times those investments become the shiniest new car in the aforementioned traffic jam of the mind.

It's better, in our experience, to invest in peace of mind. Instead of heaping on more traffic, begin to build off-ramps to ease mental congestion.

Need proof it works? Let's take a look at Zappos.

Here are 10 examples of Zappos investing in the minds of their people and creating space for innovation and execution:

1. *What am I going to do about lunch today?* Zappos answers: "Enjoy our private on-campus bistro or one of the 17 kitchenettes throughout our 10-story building." It may seem a small thing, but an appetizing option that doesn't require planning time for travel and leaving the office has massive implications on productivity.

2. *Coffee. I require coffee.* Zappos answers: "Come on down to the Café! Grab you a latté and chill on the outdoor patio for a few minutes. In fact, have your next meeting out there!" Again, no travel commitment required, but also no frustration from a bad cup of coffee that may or may not have been brewed yesterday afternoon. This is premium stuff, fresh and available, complete with space to get to know your colleagues or collaborate on that next great project.

3. *Ugh. Too much lunch. Too many lattes!* Zappos answers: "Come on down to the gym! It's open twenty-four hours a day and it's fully-equipped!" Oh, and did we mention that membership is free?

Look good, feel good, save money, and be within a five-minute walk of your next meeting? Excuses removed.

4. *My brain is fried.* Zappos answers: "How about a round of mini-golf downstairs? If mini-golf isn't your thing we could try any number of awesome recreational activities—basketball, foosball, trainer-led classes... it's all here!" [**Author's Note*: Don't forget, these are actual perks offered by Zappos in an attempt to improve and simplify the lives of their team members. Consider the intention behind each and what each investment yielded in terms of ROI.***]

5. *I have so much to do today, but my wife sent me with a to-do list a mile long from home!* Zappos answers: "Give a quick shout to our concierge services— shoe shine, car wash, oil change, dry cleaning... What else is on the list?"

6. *I am totally dreading this trip tomorrow. Two flights and a four-hour layover... ugh!* Zappos to the rescue: "Stop by the employee library on your way out this afternoon! They have everything! Current best-sellers to classics and everything in between."

7. *I don't feel so hot...* Zappos says: "Take advantage of the *free* individual health insurance for employees and reduced premiums for families!"

8. *After eating lunch, drinking a latte, a round of mini-golf and that spin class, I'm beat!* Zappos says: "Have you done any actual work today?" Not really. They would probably point the employee

in the direction of the massage chairs or the nap room with sleep pods.

9. *Holiday shipping is the worst! Those lines!* No worries... Zappos has a sleigh. Visit the on-site shipping department for all of your shipping and mailing needs.

10. *I'm fresh out of cash.* The e-Bank of Zappos says: "Use your Zollars! Who needs Ben Franklin when you can have our own internal currency with our CEO's face on it?"

[**insert slow clap here**]

The tendency when you read a list like this is to just say "Well, good for Zappos," but that's not why you picked up this book. Our goal was to find an organization who was pressing the envelope on Investing in the Mind, excavate their reasoning behind their investments and then share it with you as an example of what's possible and why it's plausible.

Zappos is world-renowned for their internal culture. That culture was born of hundreds of little employee-first decisions they have made along the way. You may not be in the market for a mini-golf course, but is there someone in your community you can contract with to help in some of those concierge areas? Car maintenance? Dry cleaning? What would a more focused and more mentally and emotionally present workforce do for your productivity?

There is one other consideration to this concept of Investing in the minds of your people: responsiveness. When you meet a felt need or supply a necessary service out of genuine care and concern for your team, they take notice. You create a bond, establish trust, and make room for synergy. Any time you can hear the words "I know you didn't have to do that but you did anyway. Thank you!" coming from an employee, that's a win. A big, obstacle-moving, chasm-crossing win.

Create that moment by investing wisely in peace of mind for your team. Their newfound mental bandwidth may well become the highway of your future.

BODY: NOT JUST APPLES FOR THE TEACHERS—BOISE SCHOOL DISTRICT

Do you remember comic books? Not the glossy, computer-generated stuff of today that gets sold only in classy bookstores. We're talking about the cheap comics you would find at the grocery store and the five-and-dime stores. Before there were mega-movie franchises, there were comics and in the back of every good comic there were ads. The coolest, most amazing gadgets and gizmos any kid could ever dream of owning. Want x-ray vision like Superman? Done via these amazing glasses for the low, low price of $14.95 plus shipping and handling.

Our grown-up selves look back and wonder what in the world we were thinking. X-ray vision for $14.95?

Lasik costs thousands! But we were caught up. Having just read 20-some-odd pages of the fantastic we were convinced, if only for a moment, that if Batman could have his belt we could have our goggles. As children, there could have been no more worthy investment than the mail order superpower du jour, but as men and women, surely we are more discerning in how we steward our resources!

When it comes to Investing in the Body for purposes of Insperience, the question is simply this: how do we empower individuals to perform physically at the highest possible level? What can we do to minimize sick days? How might we increase productivity and alertness in the first hours of the morning and the hour that follows lunch? We know that how we feel, both in our bodies— physically—and *about* our bodies—emotionally—has massive implications on productivity, so how do we equip our teams to look better, feel better, and perform better?

Let's ask the Boise School District, because they seem to have figured some things out.

In 2011, the Boise School District began a wellness program for its 3,000+ employees. Under the banner of "BSD Employees" were coaches, teachers, nurses, maintenance staff, and district level staff. Fifty-eight locations, the majority of which are populated with children and their little germ-infested hands.

The goals set out for the multi-year program were comprehensive:

- Improve employee health behaviors
- Lower elevated health risks
- Prevent chronic diseases
- Curb rising healthcare costs.

Because they understood that, for lasting change to take place buy-in was required at home, the program was extended to spouses and retirees. Due to the sheer number of participants and the breadth of a workforce spread throughout the city and region, every component of the program could be streamed to any mobile device or computer and was available in multiple languages. The first year of this initiative saw a 66% participation rate, which is pretty strong by "get in shape" program standards, but between 2011 and 2014 that number increased to 81%.

Did you catch that? A health initiative in a school district full of people stressed out over chasing other people's kids *increased* participation by 15% over three years. What allowed them to see a double-digit increase in participation over three years when most see a double-digit decrease in these initiatives within the first three months? The answer? Results. People looked better, felt better, and performed better, and that's contagious. The BSD can show tangible evidence of positive changes in behavior, improvements in biometrics associated with health risks, and boosted mental health for participants in their program. If you need hard numbers to be persuaded, a recent evaluation of six years' worth of medical claims da.a showed that participants cost significantly less than non-participants. For every dollar the Boise School District spent on wellness, it saved $3.50, and between the years of 2009 to 2014, the district experienced *no overall increase* in health care costs. From 2012 to 2014, the program participants cost the district $5,025,138 *less* in medical costs than non-participants.

Look better, feel better, perform better, save the company huge amounts of money, increase your job satisfaction. See why we love the Boise School District?

The total cost of the wellness program between 2011 and 2014 was $1.4 million. Subtract the program costs from the savings and you net $3.6 million. That buys a lot of pencils... or helps with transportation, teacher compensation, technology, and any number of other issues that plague school districts around the nation.

The district medical costs in 2014 ($11.3 million) were lower than the costs in 2009 ($11.5 million), demonstrating a zero trend across the six-year evaluation period. Why? What made this possible? The Boise School District was (a) populated with people ready and willing to make a change; and (b) led by people who were willing to invest in tools to make change possible.

It's a touchy thing, talking about health. Whether it's politically correct to point it out or not, we are witnessing an obesity epidemic in almost every major "developed nation" around the world. In 2011–2014, the same time frame of the BSD Wellness Program, middle-aged Americans (ages 40–59) had the highest obesity rate of any age group at 41.0 percent, followed by seniors (ages 60 and older) at 38.5%, and then young adults (ages 20–39) at 34.3%. Eighty percent of American adults don't meet the government's national physical activity recommendations for aerobic activity and muscle strengthening and around 45% of adults are not sufficiently active to achieve health benefits.

Reality: that last paragraph is expensive. Before you accuse us of picking on one segment of the population, we could have easily submitted equally shocking statistics for behaviors like smoking, sleep deprivation, and any number of other medically proven hindrances to good health and productivity. As difficult as these subjects may be and as much as we hesitate to be insensitive, the "personal choices" being made by members of your team are, both now and in increasing measure in the future, impacting your bottom line.

As uncomfortable as this topic may be, there is great hope on the other side of these decisions—just ask the people who were impacted by the courage of the leadership at the Boise School District. You have the opportunity to make a lasting impact on the quality of life your team enjoys, not just with respect to their productivity but also in their personal lives.

Invest well.

Chapter 8

Reward

In 1992, Dr. Gary Chapman published his book *The Five Love Languages: How to Express Heartfelt Commitment to Your Mate.* The concept was this: everyone speaks one of five specific languages when it comes to expressing and receiving affirmation, love, and praise. A couple could take a test and discover their love language, which would then empower them in communicating with each other. Knowing their own love language and that of their partner, they could send messages on a "wavelength" that the other could receive.

By 2015, *Love Languages* had eclipsed the 10 million mark of units sold and it remains at the top of the *New York Times* "Love and Relationships" list of bestsellers. It has been translated into 50 languages and has spawned an entire industry of ancillary material including *The 5 Love Languages of Children* (500,000+ copies sold), and many others.

Dr. Chapman's work exposed us to two principles of relationship management: First, affirming one's position in a relationship is not a function of giving them a title, but of purposed daily interaction. Second, purposed daily interaction must be communicated in a way that can be perceived and received by the recipient. We can agree that the husband who looks at his wife and says "I married you! I provide for you! That should be enough!" is most likely sleeping on the couch. Why, then, are so many in the marketplace willing to say to their employees "I hired you! I pay you! That should be enough"?

Enough for what? Enough to stick around? Enough to wear a title? The idea of purposed daily interaction goes both ways. It requires an employee who is willing to examine and learn what contributes to the company's culture over and above "their job" and a company culture that identifies and rewards those behaviors over and above their paycheck.

The concept of reward denotes a response to something over and above what is required. The fundamental element of reward is exchange, but we limit ourselves if we see reward only in monetary terms. That keeps us stuck on "I pay you. You work." What, then, is required to make the concept of "reward" a measurable element of your Insperience?

1. Know your team beyond titles and job descriptions. Don't get caught in old ruts of past incentives and trinkets, but take the time to learn what motivates and affirms them. A reward without value in the eyes of the recipient is hardly a reward.

2. Help your team identify behaviors that advance your cause. Help them visualize the target so that their efforts are directly in line with your ends.

Willing employees who engage in aimless attempts to get ahead are doomed to frustration.

3. Be consistent in edifying and rewarding those who go "above and beyond." Honor excellence, but beware. Rewards become entitlements when they become separated from the exchange.

Let's take a quick moment and unpack the notion of entitlements. Entitlement indicates that what is being received is based upon rights or a legal claim. Reward is achievement or merit based. Entitlement says, "You must give," where reward says, "I choose to give."

Subtle distinctions like these are precisely why rewards require discernment. Reward programs that are allowed to become stale lose their efficacy or often become entitlements. The remedy? Keep your programs fresh and in season. Keep them aimed and associated with clearly defined goals and allow those members of your team who are willing to separate from the pack and take hold of "more."

Dee Hock, the founder of Visa, said it this way:

> It is essential to employ, trust, and reward those whose perspective, ability, and judgment are radically different from yours. It is also rare, for it requires uncommon humility, tolerance, and wisdom.

Consider what this is saying. Rewards are not just trinkets passed from a superior to a supplicant. There is an underlying social component as well—the "uncommon humility, tolerance, and wisdom" piece to which Mr. Hock refers. A reward in a business is an indication of value beyond the scope of your current station. It says, effectively, that leadership recognizes that we have accomplished _____ because of your contribution.

"Without you, we wouldn't have _____."

What motivates your team? Gifts? Public praise? Time? Dr. Chapman identified the five love languages, but it's up to us to discover the native tongue of the people we seek to reward.

News flash: thinking about giving a gift or reward is not what's meant by "the thought that counts." What counts is the thought and discernment that went into offering a reward that honors the recipient according to their language.

> "Don't get caught in old ruts of past incentives and trinkets, but take the time to learn what affirms and motivates your team."

The heights to which your enterprise will climb will be determined not just by the diversity of thought and experience of the team that you employ, but how you make them feel on a daily basis. When members of your team discover innovative solutions or take risks to refine old systems, honor them! Find reasons to reward them publicly and privately and watch your ceiling rise.

HEART: BECAUSE IT MATTERS TO YOU— GOOGLE

A heartfelt reward will be met with a heartfelt response. Heartfelt rewards done extremely well are most often met with stunned silence. We once attended the annual distributor meeting for a large direct-sales company at which one of the vice presidents, having been with the company almost from the beginning, received an honorary award that he had no idea was coming. The few times this particular award had been given in the past he had been the one handing out the hardware, so how they managed to keep this secret from him no one seems to know. But seeing his response in that moment was a thing of true beauty.

Have you ever been a part of one of those moments? It's a unique moment of relational magic.

Connecting your people to the heart of your company (read: *ethos*) happens best and most naturally when you have first connected with and somehow enhanced the things which matter most to them.

A stellar benefits package is one way that companies evidence concern for their people and their people's loved ones. Along those lines, Google certainly inspires a great deal of loyalty with their team members' spouses.

If a member of the Google team—known as a "Googler"—passes away, all of their stock vests immediately, which is awesome, but then on top of the life insurance payout Google ensures that their surviving spouse continues to get half of the Googler's salary for the next ten years. There's also an additional $1,000 per month benefit for any of the Googler's children.

"When I mentioned this benefit to my wife, she cried. She actually cried that the company would do that for her if something happened to me." This is an actual quotation from a Google employee! How many companies evidence that level of esteem and honor for the families of their employees? The question "Who does this?" is fairly asked, at which point Google can raise their hand and say "We do!"

Perhaps the idea of a death benefit is a bit much. What about something more day to day? Something more practical? Google's answer comes in the form of man's best friend. Yep. Bring your dog to work. One Googler had this to say about his canine colleague: "Though managing a dog between meetings can sometimes be challenging, having her with me meant that every few hours I needed to get outside and take a break which helped me manage my energy. In addition, my dog brought a lot of spontaneous joy to my colleagues who sometimes sought her out when needing a break from an arduous task. Eventually my dog became far better known than I was and she, oddly enough, ended up introducing me to a lot of people I wouldn't have otherwise met."

You may be sitting at the desk of your ambulatory surgical center and thinking, "I don't think we're allowed to bring dogs into surgery," but be sure to grasp the spirit behind what Google is doing.

Google is speaking to the heart! Whether it's a Fall Festival where you invite your team to bring the kids and enjoy inflatables and ponies in the parking lot or a company tailgating event before the local Friday night football game, find something that allows you to touch those who matter most to your team!

One last Google-inspired consideration: for many years, Google had their own variation of the 80/20 rule. In 2007, Googlers were encouraged to dedicate 80% of time spent in the office to their primary job, and 20% working on "passion projects" that they believed would help the company. This was a reflection of Google's bent towards innovation, but consider the message it sent to their engineers. This is empowerment! This is one of the largest companies in the world saying, "We brought you here because you're one of the best. We know you have great ideas." From this company policy and best practice came some of their greatest and best-known products.

Rewarding the heart is personal, and Google found a way to remind their people that to be a Googler is to be a trusted, empowered, and inspired innovator.

Done well, rewarding the heart will become a continuum. It begins when your team sees a way to honor what matters most to them—for example, cash bonuses to pay for vacations. The loved ones of your team members will, because of the honor and generosity you show your employee, love the fact that they are affiliated with your brand. Proud moms and dads will tell their friends about little Billy's amazing job—even though "Little Billy" is now 42. Will, as he now prefers to be called, becomes more convinced every day that the hours and intellectual treasures he parts at work are not wasted in exchange for a paycheck, but invested in a place that honors him as a part of the team and a member of the larger community.

If you were to survey the family members of your team members, what would they say about how well you know, honor, and reward what matters most for their loved ones?

MIND: DOPAMINE AND YOUR BOTTOM LINE—THE MOTLEY FOOL

If we told you that you could implement a simple discipline that would have a significant impact on your team's memory, workplace efficiency, behavior and cognition, attention, sleep, mood, and learning, would we have your attention?

If so, answer this question: How much do you know about dopamine?

Quick biology refresher: dopamine is a chemical found in the brain, commonly called a neurotransmitter. Our brains use neurotransmitters to tell our hearts to beat, our lungs to breathe, and our stomachs to digest, but they also affect mood, sleep, concentration, and weight.

Dopamine, specifically, is the "feel good" neurotransmitter. When dopamine levels are high, you can expect enhanced concentration, boosted moods, and what sociologists call "pro-social" behaviors.

If you're looking to reward the mind, you're looking for ways to spike dopamine. In fact, one of the greatest ways *to* spike dopamine is through recognition and reward. So, what would happen if you had an office full of people whose dopamine levels were high? What might that dopamine boost do to productivity and ethos? Let's ask the team at the Motley Fool about their experience.

First, let's establish that the Motley Fool's employee culture is unique, and the stuff of legend. Spend some time on their website, specifically the "Workplace Culture Blog," and you'll see that they get a *lot* right when it comes to Insperience! The reason? They listen. It was in the course of listening that the leadership team at the Motley Fool began hearing via engagement surveys about issues surrounding recognition.

Specifically, recognition was too closely tied to titles...the approach too top-heavy. Why should public recognition and praise flow only from above? The team wanted to be able to publicly praise their peers for work well done. Hence was born the Motley Fool's "Golden Hall of Awesome."

Through a partnership with "You Earned It," a public news feed was set up, sending out notifications throughout the day of peers praising, edifying, and encouraging peers. To make things even more fun, points were awarded to those receiving praise for their work, which could be traded for prizes ranging from trinkets to trips. One unforeseen benefit described by leadership was the impact the program had on those who were *giving* the praise. They described it as "happy to give, happy to get!"

Employees adopted the program with enthusiasm straight out of the gate, resulting in over 13,000 posts in the first year. That equates to 35 encouraging posts per day!

Why would a seemingly simple initiative like this matter? After all, Motley didn't create it. They just employed an existing tool that was in the marketplace...no great innovation or investment on their part.

Here's why it matters:

- When asked what leaders could do more of to improve engagement, 58% of respondents replied, "give recognition" (Psychometrics).
- Companies with recognition programs that are highly effective at improving employee engagement have 31% lower voluntary turnover (Bersin & Associates).
- Forty-one percent of companies that use peer-to-peer recognition have seen positive increases in customer satisfaction (Globoforce).

- Sixty-nine percent of employees would work harder if they felt their efforts were better appreciated (Socialcast).

Rewarding the mind (read: spiking the dopamine) results in measurable rewards for the bottom line. If you'd like one more statistic, consider this: according to Bersin & Associates, 87% of existing recognition programs focus on tenure.

Translation: employees have to stick around for seven years to get an "atta boy." Worse yet, this means that *at best,* 13% of existing programs recognize daily excellence and persistence. Couple that with what the Motley Fool found to be true of themselves— recognition held under lock and key in corner offices— and you will find the reason for dopamine levels on the sales floor suffering.

Allow us to remind you, courtesy of a list from *Mental-HealthDaily.com,* what it looks like when the mind is not rewarded with Dopamine:

- Attention deficits
- Anxiety
- Cognitive impairment
- Confusion
- Depersonalization
- Depression
- Fatigue
- Lack of motivation

- Learning problems
- Poor concentration
- Inattentiveness
- Social withdrawal.

The list actually continues, but you get the point. To create an internal culture that complements our physiology and brain chemistry, recognition and praise must be present, consistent, and genuine.

Here's an assignment for you.

If the decision to get intentional about rewarding the mind through recognition could impact your employee engagement and voluntary turnover rate by 15 percent—half of the stated figure in the data we collected—how much money would you save per year?

BODY: REWARDS THAT CREATE RESULTS—REI

Have you ever tried to negotiate with a child? All parents reach a point where they finally say, "If you will just get in your bed and stay there, I will _____."
This is the point where knowing your child is really important, because if you offer the wrong thing as an incentive all credibility is lost and the negotiations start all over. Offer a kid sprouts if he'll stay in the bed and you have guaranteed yourself company for the foreseeable future.

Rewards that don't begin with the recipient in mind are tantamount to seeds spread upon concrete. They just don't produce the intended result.

As an employer, do you know what motivates your people? What makes them come alive and dream? What stimulates both the imagination and the critical "How can I make this happen" parts of their minds? The better you are at answering those questions, the more likely you will be to offer rewards that yield results.

Every friend group has that one friend who is the outdoor enthusiast. Their answer for everything is "Let's get outside!"—which means they would fit perfectly into our next featured company.

When it comes to rewarding the body, nobody does it quite like REI. REI's perks aren't all kayaks and hiking boots. When the company does well, their people do well.

How? The company's profit-sharing plan, where each year team members take home an extra five to fifteen percent of their base pay. Twice a year, REI employees get a paid day off to get outside or volunteer. To encourage continuing education the company provides tuition reimbursement. REI leadership is also thinking about their employees and their commute. Employees who utilize public transportation can get 50% of their costs covered. Those who prefer to ride bike, run, or walk to work have access to bike lockers, towels, showers, and storage in almost every REI location.

Employees also love the "Employee Grant Challenge" which gives them the funds they need for a challenging outdoor adventure and an awesome employee discount program on things they would buy anyway—50% discounts on REI gear and apparel, 30% off vendor merchandise, and 10% off sale items.

When it comes to personnel, REI isn't looking for just any guy off the street to be on their sales floor or behind the desk. They know that people who love the outdoors want to learn from and be engaged by knowledgeable people who also love the outdoors. Their clientele can smell urban from a mile away! So what do you do? You hire people who love what you stand for, use what you sell, and share a passion with your target market. From boots to headlamps these aren't just things REI employees sell, these are tools they use and swear by.

We began this chapter by asking what makes your people come alive? What stirs their imaginations and their willingness to create opportunities? Having established those answers, immerse them in it. Surround them as best you can with those elements those elements in the form of artwork and environment, then paint vision for them that will inspire them to reach beyond the standard. Isn't that what REI has done?

Think about it. They hired people who love the idea of REI, surrounded them with tools and toys they are passionate about, awarded them with product discounts and paid days to engage the community and nature, then finally *rewarded* them when the team does well in the form of profit sharing. It's as though the leadership says at every stage "We get you!"

Rewarding the body, helping your team find and enjoy some form of life/work balance is about the adjustments you make to a physical environment and system of incentives based upon a relational connection you took the time to establish.

Walk through your office today. What elements might you say would constitute an intentional effort to create a space that rewards your people for being a part of your company? Is every design element simply out of the playbook of functionality, practicality, and profitability?

Seriously, put this book down and try this!

Better yet, call three or four employees to walk through the office with you and get their thoughts on the atmosphere in which they spend half of their waking lives! Having considered the office space, let's take a look at your benefits. Are there perks that make room for and evidence your appreciation of their life outside the cubicle?

Flash forward to the time when you have done your due diligence and identified a few changes or additions you can make to reward your team. Put yourself in the office on that Monday morning when they come in to find the space re-engineered with them in mind. Picture them coming to your door to tell you what they did with the time they were offered by the company to volunteer or serve their community.

Rewarding your people, when done well, is a joy. Seeing their response is the first of the benefits you will enjoy. The next benefit comes when they respond to your intentional, purposed effort with renewed dedication and excellence in their contribution to the mission of your enterprise.

Chapter 9

Engage

How do you milk a cone snail? You might think that's the wrong question. You might be asking, "Why would you *want* to milk a cone snail?"

We promise we have a great reason for asking.

Back in 2003, renowned psychiatrist and environmentalist Eric Chivian of Harvard University described the cone snail as having "the largest and most clinically important pharmacopoeia of any genus in nature." It's been speculated that each of the cone snail's eight hundred-plus species has easily 1,000 peptides of medical interest, which means cone snails offer millions of research possibilities.

In 2004, we saw the first marketable evidence of Chivian's conjecture. The pain reliever Prialt became the first FDA-approved, commercially available product derived from cone snail toxin. This pain reliever is estimated to be 1,000 times stronger than morphine, but without addictive side effects.

Now, before you send the kids out to collect cone snails, there are a few things you need to know. These aren't garden snails. They're typically found in warm and tropical seas all over the world. They are also unbelievably venomous and capable of "stinging" humans. The sting from the barb of a small cone is no worse than a garden-variety bee sting, but that of the larger species can be fatal.

What does this have to do with engagement? Consider the path that led to the discovery, which led to the cure hidden inside the cone snail. Had the explorers remained on the surface, the story ends. As the snails live under the surface of the seas, the discovery required *depth*. Had they snorkeled recreationally and enjoyed the snail as one of many wonders under the sea, the story ends. The discovery demanded knowledge, discernment, and *focus*. The medicinal properties of the snail lie within the toxin. Had they dropped the snail at first sting, the story ends. The discovery demanded *courage*. The absence of depth, focus, and courage would have eliminated the possibility of discovering the cures hidden inside cone snail toxin. We would argue that, when it comes to engaging your team, the same three principles apply.

In any relationship, engagement is a process of discovery. Let's consider something as simple as office interactions between team members. Between the sales manager's office and her morning cup of coffee in the break room lies the sales floor, where her team of twenty-four direct reports are housed in cubicles. She can easily plot a "path of least resistance" between her door and the coffee pot, but the decision to avoid engagement with her assigned team on the floor (read: *avoid depth*) ends the story.

No trust is created, no compassion or hope displayed, no vision painted.

She will manage. Employees will be employed. End of story. The opportunity didn't require stopping at each of the twenty-four desks, only her availability. Her availability creates the opportunity for an encounter. Something as simple as a warm greeting and the courtesy of acknowledgment can transform a sales floor, but the floor won't come to you. The decision must be made to engage. This is depth.

The decision of the sales manager to engage the sales floor (depth) creates the opportunity for her to identify strengths and threats within her team or their shared environment. It is when she is intentionally interacting with those in her charge that she is afforded the opportunity to identify and direct her focused attention to challenges and opportunities. The closer you get, the clearer the picture becomes. Focus improves with proximity.

Does it require courage? Absolutely. The decision to position herself among her team through depth and focus guarantees that she will be exposed to all of the emotions that accompany "life" happening. The good news, however, is that the impact of "life happening" on the sales floor won't catch her by surprise when she sees performance statistics at week's end. The break-up in desk number nine that threatened an entire day's productivity may become the engagement opportunity that leads to identifying and endearing the company's culture to a future leader. People trust those in whom they perceive stability, and the decision of a leader to be "in the trenches" speaks volumes. The decision to enter the trenches when you could lead from a desk is courageous, and it is rewarded with loyalty.

Engagement is discovery. Call it research, if you must, but don't for a moment think that it isn't reflected in your sales reports, attrition statistics, and employee satisfaction reviews. Remember this: engagement and discovery begin with listening and observing, not necessarily moving the chess pieces. Engage your people with passion and patience as you never know when you might find the next "cone snail" who was no more than 50 feet away from you the entire time.

> "In any relationship, engagement is a process of discovery."

HEART: THE LAW OF DUPLICATION—LEE COMPANY

Why do we so often sound exactly like our parents, even to the point of saying the exact things they used to say—which we swore we would never say? The answer stems from engagement of the heart. In a healthy family environment parents establish foundations for behavior and belief upon which children build their lives. Dad's old sayings and the way your mom held her mouth when she was frustrated—you know you've caught yourself making that face—become behavioral DNA. The parent/child dynamic is evidence of a trusted provider's character and characteristics overflowing onto and into their charge. Engagement of the heart leads to duplication.

Understand that duplication is not mimicry, nor is it an attempt to replicate the original. It has more to do with recognizable traits and fundamental elements from the previous generation manifesting themselves in the next. The magic is that these traits are passed on and evident, but they don't compromise the uniqueness of the next generation.

As you may have guessed, this isn't just a physiological proposition. Duplication takes place in the world of business every single day as mindsets, methods of operation, and core beliefs are passed through generations of industry and enterprise. To simplify: employees do what they see leadership do. Mission and vision statements notwithstanding, they will live out in their work what they see their leadership living out.

Lee Company in Nashville, Tennessee, is one of those companies that it's hard to find anyone willing to criticize. It's been around since 1944, passing from generation to generation of the Lee family, and serves as the largest mechanical contractor in Tennessee. With over 1,200 employees, you'll hear them described as home and residential "fix everything from HVAC to plumbing and electrical" friends of the community.

Were you to look on the "About Us" tab of their website, you would find their mission statement and vision to be simple and honest—the standard by which they conduct their business. Lee Company is known for providing excellent service to homes and businesses of all sizes, from the smallest family home to the home of the NHL's Nashville Predators on Broadway, but there is an affection for Lee that goes beyond their service excellence. Even among its competitors, Lee Company is held in high esteem.

Why? What makes them special? You already know the answer. It's the people. Moreover, it's the atmosphere their people create.

Lee Company is known to be generous to the community. From being among the largest supporters of Nashville's Second Harvest Foodbank to supporting other charities throughout Tennessee and Northern Alabama, Lee and Lee's people show up to serve. It surprised no one when a team of their technicians mobilized to go to the hurricane-ravaged parts of Texas after Hurricane Harvey.

People would say, "Of course... that's just Lee!" But it wasn't. Lee Company didn't send them. It was Lee employees who asked for unpaid time off to go and serve. The company made a contribution towards their trip, but Lee didn't send them. They were just behaving like Lee. There are two inescapable realities to human behavior:

- *Culture trickles down.* When you consider what it means to engage the heart of your team, you will find that your culture and your cultural values will ultimately be a reflection of your leadership. It would be easy if that meant everyone would behave like the CEO, but leadership is bestowed level after level throughout an organization. Picture it as champagne glasses stacked in a pyramid, all being filled by overflow from the level above. One glass that contains contents unintended overflows into every glass below. So, what does your team see and receive from the level above them, from maintenance to management and into the C-Suite? Duplication says that what they see and receive they will pass on because culture trickles down.
- *Fire Burns Up.* If you were in a twenty-story building in which floors eight through eleven were on fire, where would you want to be—other than outside? Above the fire or below? The answer is below. Why? Because fire burns up. This principle also extends to culture. Whether the fire is passion for good work or anger about working conditions, a fire which begins among the employed masses will make its way to the empowered few.

What's the lesson here? Engaging the heart is not a program or a mandate. Nor is it behavior modification. Leaders engage the heart by proximity and visibility—being seen doing the things which you would see your team duplicate.

Employees who are cared for extend care.

Employees who are served well offer excellent service.

This is the nature of behavioral duplication.

We began by talking about the reality that, no matter how much we may protest, we sometimes sound like our parents. When kids act out, the first place we look is to the home for understanding. Let us be clear that not all bad behavior in children is the fault of the parents. Similarly, not every broken piece of corporate culture is the fault of poor management, but the solution in each case is found in engaging the heart. Behaviors can be manipulated, but culture is won at the heart level.

Duplication is real. How we respond to difficulty and challenges will say as much as how we celebrate our victories. How your leadership begins their meetings will inform how your employees begin their workdays. Is leadership reacting or responding? Reactive or proactive?

The apple doesn't fall far from the tree.

MIND: MANAGING THE SENSES—ASANA

Imagine if you went home today and told your family that you will be celebrating Christmas this year with no

Christmas music, no tree, no decorations, no holiday-themed parties, and no ugly Christmas sweaters. How different would the month of December be for you? How would it impact your anticipation of Christmas morning? Would your kids wake you up at 4:37 a.m. and rush downstairs to see what had been left for them under the recliner?

Christmas has an atmosphere that we actually experience. All of our senses are tuned during that time of year towards celebrating the holidays, which means that Christmas remains top of mind until the last gift is opened and the last decoration has been stowed away. If you alter the Christmas atmosphere you alter the experience. The Christmas season and all of its sensory overload has mastered the art of engaging the mind.

Have you ever tried to work on a project with a hard deadline in the completely wrong environment? By "wrong environment," we mean the wrong environment for you to maximize your efforts. The local coffee shop, for instance, can be for one person a place of inspiration while simultaneously being a place of immense distraction for another. When it comes to engaging the mind, physical atmosphere is everything. As an element of your Insperience, this is creating a space where the fundamental elements of your enterprise—things like creativity, productivity, and community—are intentionally heightened.

What ethos must you intentionally create to attract the right people to your team, empower them to exceed expectations, and connect on a personal level with their work and coworkers?

Allow us to introduce Asana.

Asana is a cloud-based project management system whose mission is "to help humanity thrive by enabling all teams to work together effortlessly." Asana exists to allow companies large and small to take their many moving parts and put them into a single place where project participants can enjoy clear communication, tasks, timelines, and every pertinent detail at the click of a button.

The first litmus test of a company which exists to enable other companies to "enjoy working together effortlessly" is a quick assessment of their own culture. Are they enjoying what they say they create for others? The answer is an emphatic "Yes!"

Asana began humbly, with around fifty people crammed into one floor of a nondescript office building in San Francisco. Within three years, they exploded to over 240 people in San Francisco alone with offices in New York and Dublin. As they grew, Asana made one pivotal decision that they credit above all others with establishing the atmosphere that permeates their work: they employed and empowered their facilities team. Specifically, they tasked the facilities team with this phrase: "Growth without growing pains."

Tasked with what some would say was the impossible, the Team went to work establishing some "non-negotiables" that continue to guide their work to this day. Let's look at a few:

1. *Minimize disruptions.* How productive would you be tomorrow if you found out, upon entering the office, that you were going to have to move offices on Thursday morning at ten? Or, instead of moving offices, there would be a six-week construction project starting tomorrow that would be taking place just next door. Hammers, drills, and saws would be your workday serenade, but "It's only for a few weeks." This didn't happen at Asana. The facilities team committed to evening and weekend work, especially for heavy construction projects. Did it cost more? In terms of hourly work, the answer is yes, but imagine what they saved in productivity. Their intellectual momentum wasn't compromised by the physical distractions of progress.

2. *Café Narwhal.* You read that right. The facilities team at Asana was *all about* soliciting input and buy-in for the teams for whom they were creating an environment. A "Brainstorm Board" was installed on the main floor, soliciting input on how they could keep the flow of the office connected as they expanded to multiple floors. Imagine the excitement of the Asana team seeing their visions and suggestions made a reality. Why assign some generic name for your in-house espresso bar and conference rooms when you are surrounded by creatives? "Welcome to Café Narwhal!" Imagine the smiles on their faces every time that simple phrase touches their ears. The facilities team understood

the power of ownership and involvement in the process of creating an engaging atmosphere.

3. *Consistency.* Anywhere you are in the world that is owned and run by Asana *looks and feels* like Asana. Whether you wander from floor to floor of the San Francisco office, or you fly from the Dublin office to New York, you will be welcomed and immersed by the familiar. Don't mistake "familiar" for boring, however. Asana used the same designer to lay out and furnish each office, the same hand-lettered meeting room signs. Asana makes "familiar" look fabulous, and their people love it.

4. *Flow.* Forgive us for sounding like something off of HGTV, but open floor plans matter when you're talking about creative people. Because one of the pillars of Asana's success is collaboration, they built into each office space what they call "soft areas" with couches, tables, and board games. They made sure that each floor contained common spaces where their team can enjoy being and innovating together. Asana gets that fully one-third of their employees' lives are spent at work. A special team deserves a special space.

Growth without growing pains. Physical progress that doesn't stall intellectual momentum. Creating an atmosphere that complements their very intentional culture. All of this Asana does in an effort to engage the minds of their team. They take every opportunity to appeal to the senses of their employees, both physical and emotional. Add to all of this the unlimited vacation days and a six-week sabbatical after three years of working with the company and you begin to see why Asana's employees are "all in." Why would they ever be otherwise?

The physical environment within your office necessarily impacts the physical senses of your employees. Jot down the five senses on a piece of paper—sight, smell, touch, taste, and hearing—then walk through your office and write down what you experience. Take a day and sit in one of the chairs you provide for your team and see how comfortable you are by day's end. Trade your fancy coffee for something from the break room for a few days. Work from a cubicle and see how many distractions contend for your attention. It's hard to do good work when your back hurts from an old chair, your coffee tastes funky and your cubicle mate is reenacting the drum solo from "Wipe Out" all day every day. Add to that the grey walls and shuttered windows and you have a recipe for poor productivity.

Engaging the Mind requires managing the senses!

BODY: INSPIRATION & INNOVATION IN ACTION—RED FROG EVENTS

Engagement is, by definition, active, which means it has become a little unnatural for many people. So familiar are we with instant and constant access to every basic need that we have lost some of our primal instincts.

Hunger no longer stirs us to plant or hunt. Loneliness no longer stirs us to leave the house. Choose your favorite activity: cooking, fishing, losing weight, exploring the wilderness, throwing a ball. When did we stop doing and start watching? Our bodies are no longer primed to perform tasks beyond pushing a gas pedal and lifting a fork, so how do we change course?

Red Frog Events offers the solution—*stop watching and start doing.*

Here's what they did.

In 2007, founder Joe Reynolds took his affinity for watching people race around the world and created what he called "The Great Urban Race" in Illinois. As it turned out, he wasn't the only one ready to run. One hundred and fifty-six people turned out for the first event, which led to seven more Urban races in the first year. In 2008, Urban Races started spreading around the country and event coordinators began coming on board with Joe's vision. The year 2009 saw the first ever "Warrior Dash," which sold out almost immediately with over two thousand participants. Red Frog Events was on the move, adding staff and building a culture which emphasized and empowered "doing." By 2015, the Warrior Dash had hosted over 2.5 million participants at events hosted all over the world.

Perhaps jumping through fire and muddy obstacle courses aren't your thing. Would you like to dance? Check out the Red Frog's Firefly Music Festival. What began as a concert event in Dover, Delaware, with forty bands in

2012, exploded in popularity almost instantly. By 2014, the event boasted over 120 bands on seven stages. And by 2015, the event was selling out with a whopping 90,000 attendees. Why is Red Frog so great at getting people off the couch and into action? Spend some time on their website and you will see it immediately. Consider this excerpt from "*What Makes Us, Us?*"

> While all of our employees come from different backgrounds, we have a few things in common: we're kind-hearted, team players to the core, and we love to laugh. What makes an ideal Red Frogger isn't years of experience or number of events planned—it's the ability to lead, innovate, and laugh when you're thrown into new situations every day. It's the ability to create remarkable work, world-class events, and lasting friendships with a team of hard-working people that have a common goal in mind.

Study the many manifestations of their passion—the Chicago Beer Classic, ShamrockFest, the Big Barrel Country Music Festival, and on and on the list goes. You will see this mission reflected in everything they do. How does that passion to get people up and actively engaged translate into such explosive growth in seemingly everything they touch? How does that fun-loving culture breed such excellence?

Credit the Red Frog Way:

We boldly aspire to make a positive impact on the world, be the crown jewel of our industry, and stay healthy and thriving for 100+ years. Bringing this vision to life takes passionate people and a shared way that unites us. We call it our "Red Frog Way" and it's the secret sauce that leads us onward and upward.

Heart—it begins with kindness at our core. We do the right thing and give back in a big way.

Grit—we rise to the occasion. With resilience and contagious optimism, we push forward.

Entrepreneurial Spirit—ask "why." Dream big. Dive in. Make mistakes. Repeat.

Red Frog Proud—those soak-it-in moments when it all comes together.

Frog Family—road trips, growing pains, occasional cry laughs—when you laugh so hard you cry—and not letting each other fail. That's why we call ourselves family.

[_____]—our last way celebrates individuality. After all, we're each as unique as a Panamanian red frog.

Perhaps you're thinking that, while all of this is great for Red Frog, your line of work is a little less... fun-loving. It's easy to excuse ourselves from this level of boldness and freedom to passionately pursue things like "fun" because, after all, someone has to **insert comparatively mundane task here**— but there is a timeline in their story that is easy to overlook.

We're holding Red Frog up as the poster child for engaging the body, but none of the Red Frog story would have ever happened had their founder not been inspired—an engagement of the heart—by what he saw others enjoying on television. That inspiration led him to innovation—engaging the mind—and the creation of the Urban Race, which was the genesis of the Warrior Dash and everything else that followed.

Inspiration (Heart) led to innovation (Mind), which created action (Body). That action served as an inspiration to others which led to further innovation and created more action. For Red Frog, that wheel continues to turn over again and again because the culture embraces and celebrates each turn. Remove any part of the equation and the process shuts down completely.

Engaging the body is active. It is inspiration and innovation in action. Whether you build software or crunch numbers for a living, inspiration is everywhere and in every industry. Find it, cultivate it, and celebrate it among your staff and watch your team rise. And if you have occasion to enjoy a team-building exercise at a Warrior Dash near you we strongly recommend it.

Bring your Viking helmet.

PART 3

PUTTING INSPERIENCE INTO ACTION

Chapter 10

Capstone to the Journey: Putting Insperience into Action

We began this book with a simple question—where do we begin? Having set the destination as a transformation of your internal culture, where does the journey begin and what directional signs mark the path?

We invited you to follow a path that leads to enlightenment, enhancement, and change. Whether you reach your final destination will be the product of the paths you choose, the detours you make, and the experiences you encounter along the way. You may have finished the book, but your journey has just begun.

We established that every encounter creates an experience, an impression, and ultimately a mindset for and within the receiving party. You've challenged yourself by asking this question: "Are we causing positive experiences for the people within our organization?"

The honest answer to that question is truly where your journey begins.

At every turn along this journey, you had an opportunity to consider the internal experiences you are causing on a daily basis. Critical and frequent analysis of this seemingly simple discipline of "treating people well" will allow your organization to reach relational, fiscal, and even personal milestones that you never thought possible. You now have the necessary ingredients to begin to build an internal experience—an Insperience—that will be transformative for your organization and for the lives of your people.

Insperience is more than an employee engagement buzzword. It affects every piece of the relevance, wellness and fiscal viability of an organization. It inspires cultural transformation from the inside out.

Thank you for sharing this journey with us. We are excited for you to dig down to the very foundations of your organizational culture and to establish a mindset of simply treating each other better. Creating positive encounters and committing to an Insperience can become the cornerstone of continued growth and prosperity for your organization and your people.

Remember this: there is never a bad time to enhance your culture. We would remind you to utilize the Insperience Quotient as your compass for the journey ahead.www.expquest.com

Begin now to build your Insperience, employing the I.N.S.P.I.R.E. road map with intentional focus on the Heart, Mind, and Body of your people.

It's time to begin.

It's time to do the good work and receive the very real benefits of treating people better.

We want to sincerely thank you for coming along with us on this journey.

About the Authors

Brian T. Church is an international best-selling author, a syndicated radio show host, and a globally recognized speaker with over 15 years of experience on the platform. Over his career, Brian has founded myriad companies, including Ambassadors International, an Executive Level Consulting Firm, Experience Global, a Customer Experience Analytics and Training company as well as TheStartup.com, the world's first completely Virtual Startup Incubator.

Phillip Duncan is a critically acclaimed trainer and motivational speaker, with a special emphasis on what he calls "Purpose Excavation." From successes in real estate and the direct selling industry, to his current role in Partnership Development, his gift lies in helping others exhume and express passion. Phillip, his wife Mary Alice, and their four sons live in Nolensville, Tennessee.